To: Jackson George

From:

Mrs. Darby
Mrs. Loveless
St. Paul Nursery School
2015

My First Bible Storybook
This edition published 2011 by Concordia Publishing House
3558 South Jefferson Avenue · St. Louis, MO 63118-3968

www.cph.org · 1-800-325-3040

Originally published under the title: *"My First Bible Storybook"* by Copenhagen Publishing House, Denmark
Copyright © 2009 Copenhagen Publishing House

Illustrated by Jacob Kramer
Retold by Michael Berghof
Designer: David Lund Nielsen

ISBN 978-0-7586-2729-2

Printed in China

China/ 019253/ 408863

My First

Bible
Storybook

The Old Testament

The Story of Creation   7

Adam and Eve   15

The Fall   28

Noah's Big Boat   39

The Rainbow   44

The Big Tower of Babel   51

God Chooses Abraham   55

A Wife for Isaac   61

Jacob and Esau   65

Jacob's Dream   70

Jacob Meets Esau   74

Joseph the Dreamer   77

Joseph in Prison   82

From Prisoner to Leader in Egypt   85

Joseph's Brothers in Egypt   91

Moses in the Basket   98

Moses and the Burning Bush   103

The Ten Plagues   108

Crossing the Red Sea   122

God's Care for the People   126

The Ten Commandments   130

Twelve Spies   134

The Walls of Jericho   137

Gideon and the Wet Wool   142

Gideon's Three Hundred Men   146

Samson the Super Strong   151

Samuel, the Boy Who
   Listened to God   158

David and Goliath   164

Saul and David   173

Solomon, the Wise King   179

Elijah, Prophet of Fire   182

The Big Test   186

The Chariot of Fire   192

Daniel's Friends in the
   Burning Fire   197

Daniel and the Lions   203

Queen Esther   210

Jonah and the Whale   216

The New Testament

Mary and Gabriel   228

Jesus Is Born in Bethlehem   233

The Wise Men   239

Jesus in the Temple   246

John the Baptist   251

"Come and Follow Me"   255

The Wedding at Cana   258

"Don't Worry about Tomorrow"   262

Through the Roof to Jesus   265

Two Fish and Five Loaves of Bread
272

Jesus Walks On Water   277

Jairus's Little Daughter   282

The Good Shepherd   286

The Lost Son Comes Home   292

The Good Samaritan Neighbor   298

The Farmer and the Good Soil   304

The Treasure and the
Beautiful Pearl   311

The Lord's Prayer   316

Lazarus, Wake Up!   318

Jesus and Children   322

Zacchaeus Was a Little Man   324

Entering Jerusalem   328

A Very Special Meal   332

In the Garden of Gethsemane   335

Jesus before the High
Priest and Pilate   338

The Cross   340

Jesus Is Alive!   342

The Big Catch of Fish   347

Jesus Leaves Earth   351

Flames of Fire   356

Peter and John in the Temple   360

When Saul Became Paul   364

Paul in Prison   370

Shipwrecked!   374

God's Wonderful City   380

The Old Testament

The Story of Creation

In the beginning, before time began, God created the universe. The earth was an empty and dark place and there was no life or light. In six days, God created the world and everything in it.

The first thing God created was the light. God said, "Let there be light." Suddenly, the first bright light began to shine in the empty earth. God saw the light was good and He named the light "day," and He called the darkness "night." This was the first day.

On the second day, God commanded the waters covering the whole earth
to pull back. God divided the earth between the dry land and the big seas.
He said, "Let dry ground rise out of the water." And so it happened. Now
the world had mountains and valleys. It had lakes and rivers.

On the third day, God said, "Let the earth be filled with green grass." He put tall trees and beautiful flowers everywhere. He filled the world with color. And God saw all He created was wonderful. This was the third day.

On the fourth day, God made the sun, the moon, and the stars. He made the sun shine from the sky during the day. At night, God made the moon to shine along with all the countless glittering stars of the universe.

But the earth was very quiet and still because no living beings had been created. Then, on the fifth day, God created fish in the seas and rivers. He also made birds to fly through the sky and among the trees while singing their happy songs. And God saw that everything He had created was good.

On the sixth day, God made animals of every kind to live on the dry land of the earth. God made every animal you can think of--from elephants and zebras to lions and cattle to sheep, dogs, and cats. He made the very largest and the very smallest creatures on earth. When God had created all this, He said, "This is really good."

God was almost finished creating the world. But there was still something important He wanted to create. God knew the most fantastic of all His creations was still to come.

Adam and Eve

On that same day God said, "Now I will create people. I will make them in My image. I will give them a conscience so they can think, know, and love Me and each other. I will make them masters of everything I have made so they can take care of it." Then God took dust from the dry land and He formed Adam, the first man.

God gave Adam his shape and breathed life through his nostrils so
Adam became alive and started to breathe like all living things do.
Adam opened his eyes and found himself in a wonderful garden, called
Eden, which God had created for him.

Adam was excited about all the many animals that were surrounding him in the Garden of Eden. And he began to give all the animals names to tell them from one another.

Adam pointed at the different animals and called them giraffe, rhinoceros, hippopotamus, kangaroo, crocodile, lion. And on he went, naming all the many animals God had brought before him.

Adam could play with the animals if he wanted. None of the animals were dangerous; they all got along. But Adam felt lonely, because among all the living beings, he did not find any that looked like him. Adam was the only human on the earth.

God saw that it was not good for Adam to be alone and said, "I will create a companion for him." So God made Adam fall into a deep sleep. God took out one of his ribs, and from it, He formed Eve. When Adam woke up from his deep sleep and opened his eyes, he saw this new person. He said, "She shall be called a woman, because she came from man."

This was the sixth day. God saw all that He had made, and He said it was very good.

From the very first moment they saw each other, Adam and Eve loved each other deeply. Adam no longer felt alone because he now could talk to someone. Eve was happy to be Adam's wife and partner.

Adam taught Eve all the names he had given the animals. She was very happy with all the beautiful things in the garden that God had made for them.

Then Adam said, "Your name will be Eve." And God blessed Adam and Eve and told them to be happy and enjoy all that He had created.

God said, "Have children and let them help you take care of everything I have created. I want all the earth to be full of life, and I want everything to prosper, blossom, and grow. You can eat whatever you find in the garden I have made for you. But do not eat the fruit of the tree of the knowledge of good and evil. If you do, you will die."

Adam and Eve took care of the garden and all the animals exactly as God had told them to. In the evening as the air cooled down, God came to them in the garden.

Everything God created was beautiful and perfect. And when His work of creation was finished, He rested. Adam and Eve rested too.

After these first six days, when time had just begun and God had created everything, He said, "Everything is perfect now. This is very, very good." It looked as if nothing could destroy the joy Adam and Eve experienced in the Garden of Eden where God had created everything so wonderful and perfect.

The Fall

Genesis 3

Then, one day, when Eve was standing near the tree of the knowledge of good and evil, she heard a voice speaking to her. It was a snake! But it wasn't just any snake.

God created all animals, and that means all animals are good. But Satan can make himself look like anything he wants to. And this time, he looked like a snake. "Did God really tell you not to eat fruit from that tree?" Satan asked Eve. "Are you sure God meant what He said?"

"Yes, I am sure God said we cannot eat fruit from this tree," Eve said.

"But are you sure you cannot have even a little bite of the fruit? It won't really hurt you," Satan tempted.

Eve could not stand the temptation. She disobeyed God. Eve took fruit from the tree, tasted it, and ate it. And she liked it.

She gave some of it to Adam, and he ate it too. But as soon as they had eaten the fruit, they felt bad. Adam and Eve knew they had sinned.

Until this moment, everything in the garden had been good. But now everything was very different. Adam and Eve were sad and ashamed for disobeying God. They also realized that they were naked, and they hid in shame.

In the evening, when God came walking through the garden, Adam and Eve did not to go out to meet Him. God knew they were hiding. So He called out, "Adam, where are you?"

"Here I am," said Adam. But he and Eve were afraid.

God knew everything they said and did, of course, but He wanted them to confess. God asked, "Did you eat the fruit I had forbidden you to eat?"

"It was Eve, the woman You gave to me." Adam said. "She made me eat the fruit." Then Eve said, "It was the evil snake that tempted me and made me eat from the tree."

Their disobedience made God angry and sad. He said, "I told you not to eat fruit from this tree. Now you cannot live in the garden. Now you must leave the Garden of Eden forever. You will have to live on the earth where you must take care of yourself. And you will no longer be able to speak with Me face-to-face like you have done here in Eden." Then God said to the serpent, "One day, Someone will defeat you."

It was a very sad day when Adam and Eve had to leave the garden. God placed an angel holding a flaming sword at the entrance to Eden. No one can ever enter the Garden of Eden again.

Noah's Big Boat

Genesis 6–9

Many years went by, and the earth was now full of people. But most people had completely forgotten about God. They did many evil things and were hateful to one another. This made God very sad, and He tried to find a good person somewhere on earth. Among all the people, God found only one good man. His name was Noah. Noah loved and obeyed God.

God said to Noah, "I am sorry that I created people, and I want to start all over again. I am going to send a big flood over the world, but you and your family will be safe."

God then told Noah to build a giant boat called an ark. It was big enough to hold Noah's family and one pair, a male and female, of all animals living on the earth.

"The ark will protect you and the animals and keep you safe from the flood," God said.

Noah and his three sons, Shem, Ham, and Japheth, spent many years building the ark. They followed God's instructions for the ark exactly. While they were building it, all their neighbors made fun of them. But Noah warned his neighbors and said God would send a flood that would destroy everything on the earth. Noah said the people should stop doing wicked things to one another and obey God instead. The people didn't listen to Noah.

When the ark was finished, God sent every kind of animal to Noah. Two by two, the animals entered the ark where rooms were prepared for them to stay. When all the animals and Noah's family were inside the ark, God Himself closed the big door to the ark.

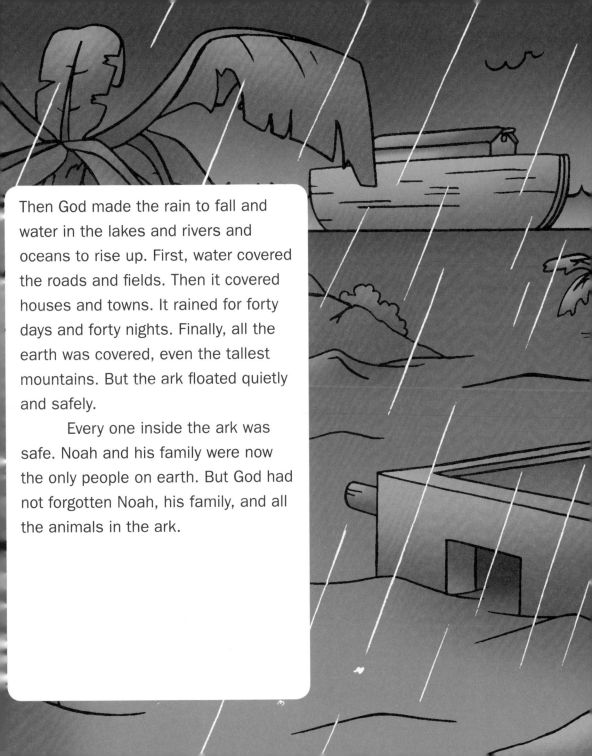

Then God made the rain to fall and water in the lakes and rivers and oceans to rise up. First, water covered the roads and fields. Then it covered houses and towns. It rained for forty days and forty nights. Finally, all the earth was covered, even the tallest mountains. But the ark floated quietly and safely.

Every one inside the ark was safe. Noah and his family were now the only people on earth. But God had not forgotten Noah, his family, and all the animals in the ark.

The Rainbow

After the rain stopped, the ark floated around on the water for months and months. The water began to dry up little by little and the mountaintops were now visible again. But all the valleys and mountains were still covered by water. Then, one day, the ark touched dry ground on the side of a mountain.

Noah opened a window in the ark and sent out a raven to see if the water had dried up from the land. The bird flew away, but it came back to the ark because it did not find any land.

Noah waited forty days, then he sent out a dove to see if there was dry land. But the dove returned to the ark because it found no place to land. Noah waited seven more days and sent the dove out again. This time it came back with a green twig in its beak. Noah smiled. He now knew that it was possible to find dry land.

A week later, Noah released the dove once more, and this time it did not return. Noah knew it was time to leave the ark. God said, "Everyone can leave the ark, for the flooding is over."

God opened the door of the ark. And Noah sent out all the animals and the people. They were excited to go out into a new world just waiting for them.

Then Noah built an altar to worship and praise God and to thank Him for keeping his family and all the animals safe. Then God blessed Noah and his sons and said, "I am making a promise to you today. See the rainbow I have put up in the sky? This shall be a sign to you that I will never again destroy the whole world with a flood."

From that day until this very day, God's people always remembered His promise to them. After the rain, when the sun was breaking through and the bright, colorful rainbow appeared in the sky, they knew that God would keep His promises. Always.

The Big Tower of Babel

Many years after the flood, the world was again full of people. Everyone spoke the same language and people from all over the world easily understood one other.

One day, many people gathered in a city. "Let us build a tall building that will reach to heaven," they said. "Then, we will always be remembered in the future as the greatest and most magnificent people who ever lived on the earth."

But the people didn't want to glorify God with this tower; they only wanted to look important. God said that if they built this tower, people would again become as wicked and selfish as they were before the great flood.

To stop their wickedness, God came and gave all of the people new languages. The groups of people became very confused because they did not understand what the others said. They could not work together anymore and had to give up their plan to build the tower.

The tower was never completed and nothing remains of it today. The city where this happened is called *Babel*, which means "confusion," because God caused their languages to be confused there.

God Chooses Abraham

Genesis 12–23

In the city of Ur, there lived a faithful man named Abraham. He was one of the world's richest men, so rich that he needed hundreds of workers to take care of all his cattle, sheep, and camels.

One day, God said to Abraham, "I want you and your wife, Sarah, to move to another country, called Canaan. I have a special plan for you and your family."

Immediately, Abraham and Sarah obeyed and began a very long journey to their new homeland. All their workers also had to follow them to help take care of all their animals and belongings.

They traveled for many years before they finally reached the land God had promised to Abraham. Their new home was now in Canaan. They put up their tents near the big trees at a place called Hebron.

Abraham loved Sarah very much. But they were sad because they had no children and now were quite old.

Then, one night God gave Abraham a new promise. He said, "Abraham, look up at the sky and see if you can count all the stars there. I promise that you will have as many children as there are stars in the sky. Your family will give the world something wonderful."

This was hard to believe, though, because Sarah was too old to have a baby. But Abraham trusted God to keep His promise.

One day, as Abraham sat outside his tent at the hottest time of the day, he looked up and saw three men close by. Abraham loved to have guests for dinner. So he asked them, "Would you like something to eat?" Sarah made them a nice dinner. And as they sat, they said something quite strange to Abraham. "Next year, at this same time, you and your wife, Sarah, will have a son."

Now Abraham knew these men came from God, and he believed what they said. But Sarah could not believe it. She laughed loudly and said to herself, "How can it be possible for me to have a baby at my age?"

God heard Sarah laughing and said, "Why did Sarah laugh? Is anything impossible for God?" God kept His promise and gave them a son exactly a year later. Abraham named the boy Isaac, which means "laughter."

A Wife for Isaac

When Isaac grew up, Abraham wanted a good wife for him. So Abraham called his most trusted servant and said, "I want you to find a wife for Isaac. Go to see my brother's family back in the country we came from and look for someone to be Isaac's wife." The servant took ten camels and started the long journey.

Finally, he reached a city called Nahor, where he stopped at a well for water because his animals were thirsty. The servant prayed to God to help him. The servant said, "When the women are coming to get water from the well, show me the girl who is the right wife for Isaac. Let it be the woman who offers to get me and the camels some water to drink."

Just then, a girl came to the well. Her name was Rebekah.

First, Rebekah offered water to the servant. Then she gave water to the camels. The servant knew God had chosen Rebekah to be Isaac's wife.

The servant gave her a ring and two bracelets. Then he asked Rebekah's father if she could marry Isaac. Rebekah's father said yes, and the next day, the servant and Rebekah traveled back to meet Isaac. Rebekah was happy to meet this young man, Isaac, about whom she had heard so many good things.

Jacob and Esau

Genesis 25–33

Isaac and Rebekah soon had two sons, named Esau and Jacob. The oldest was Esau. The youngest was Jacob. They were twin brothers but they did not look alike. Esau had long thick hair on his arms and legs. Jacob's skin was soft and smooth. When they grew older, Esau liked to live outdoors and hunt. Jacob enjoyed staying close to home.

Isaac was now very old. One day, he called his oldest son, Esau, and said, "It is time for someone else to lead the family. Take your weapons and go hunting. Bring back some meat and fix me a good meal. After the meal, I will bless you and make you the leader of our family."

Rebekah heard this, and because she loved Jacob more than Esau, she wanted Jacob to have the blessing instead. She said to him, "Go quickly and prepare some meat and put on clothes that belong to Esau." She then took hair from a small goat and put the hair on Jacob's arms to make his skin feel like Esau's.

Next, Jacob brought the meat to his father and acted as if he was Esau. When old Isaac smelled Jacob's clothes, they smelled like Esau. And when he felt Jacob's hairy arms, they felt like Esau's. So Isaac was tricked by Jacob, and he gave his blessing to Jacob instead of Esau.

Soon after this, Esau returned from his hunting. He said to Isaac, "Father, I am back and have prepared a wonderful meal for you. Now, will you give me your blessing, like you said?" But Isaac asked, "Who are you?" Esau replied, "I am your firstborn son, Esau."

Then Isaac and Esau knew that Jacob had tricked them. Esau was so angry that he said he would kill his brother.

Jacob's Dream

Genesis 28

Rebekah heard Esau's threat and warned Jacob, "You must leave now
and go and stay with your uncle, Laban, who lives in the land of Karan."
Jacob had to leave home as quickly as he could.

It was a long journey to Karan. One night, Jacob was so completely exhausted that he decided to lay down on the hard ground and use a flat stone for a pillow. Jacob fell into a deep sleep.

As he was sleeping, he had a strange dream. In this dream, he saw a ladder going up into the sky. Angels were going up and down the ladder. God stood at the top of the ladder and said to Jacob, "I will be with you, protect you, and keep you safe. I promise that you will have a family that is too big to count. And your family will give the world something wonderful."

The next morning when Jacob woke, he said, "Now I know for sure that God is with me and wants to bless me." He then took the stone he had used as a pillow and raised it up and poured oil on it. It marked the spot where God talked to Jacob in a dream.

Jacob Meets Esau

Genesis 32–33

Finally, Jacob came to Laban's house. Laban was a very rich man and owned hundreds of cows, sheep, and goats. For twenty years, Jacob worked for Laban, taking care of his animals.

Jacob married Laban's daughters and had eleven sons. Jacob also became a rich man and owned many cows, sheep, and goats.

It had been many years since Jacob had run away, but he still wanted to go home to Canaan. When Esau learned that Jacob was coming home, he sent a message to him. He told Jacob, "I am bringing four hundred men to meet you." Jacob was afraid that Esau was still very angry at him. Jacob thought, "I am afraid Esau still wants to kill me." So Jacob sent out servants to take gifts to Esau, hoping this would cause his brother to let go of his anger.

But Esau had already forgiven Jacob. He had sent the men to Jacob only to help him with his animals. When Esau saw Jacob, he ran to him and hugged him and kissed him. Although Jacob had tricked Esau and made him very angry, Esau had forgiven him and was very happy to see his brother again.

Joseph The Dreamer

Genesis 37–47

Jacob had returned to Canaan and the family was together again.

Eventually, Jacob's family grew until he had twelve sons and a daughter. Jacob's favorite son was Joseph. He made a beautiful, expensive coat for Joseph. The coat made Joseph's brothers very jealous.

Joseph had many dreams. One day, Joseph dreamed that he and his brothers were cutting stalks of grain. They tied the grain into bundles, and the brother's bundles all bowed down in front of Joseph's bundle.

Another time, Joseph dreamed that he saw the sun, the moon, and twelve stars. One of the stars was named for Joseph. And in the dream, he saw all the other stars bow down to his star.

When Joseph told his brothers about his dreams, they became angry. They said, "So, do you think it would be right for us to bow down before you, although you are our younger brother? Dream on, little brother."

And from that point, they decided they wanted to get rid of Joseph.

One day, when Joseph and his brothers were far from home, they caught him, tore off his coat, and threw him down into an empty well.

When some traveling businessmen came by, the brothers pulled Joseph up again and sold him to these men. The men took Joseph with them to Egypt, where he became a slave.

But God did not forget Joseph, and He protected him.

Joseph in Prison

Genesis 40

In Egypt, an evil woman lied about Joseph, and although he was innocent, he was put in prison. It was a dark and scary place, but even in prison, God was with him. Joseph made friends with the other prisoners. He listened carefully to them and was able to explain the meaning of their dreams.

One of the prisoners had worked closely with the king. One night, he had a dream. Then he told Joseph about it. Joseph said, "In the past, you were the king's special servant. Your dream means that you will be his servant again very soon."

Three days later, just as Joseph promised, the man was released and went back to the palace to work for the king. Joseph said to him, "Please, do not forget me. Help me get out of prison." The man promised to help, but he was so glad to be free that he forgot to tell anyone about Joseph.

From Prisoner to Leader in Egypt

Genesis 41

Two years went by and Joseph was still in prison. At that time, the king of Egypt had some very strange dreams that caused him to worry. One night, the king had a dream. He saw seven ears of corn. They were thick and full of grain, all growing on one stalk. But another stalk had seven ears that were dried up and very thin. Then the thin ears of corn ate the thick ones.

The same night the king had another dream. He was standing beside the Nile River. Suddenly, he saw seven fat, healthy cows come out of the grass along the river bank. Next, seven skinny cows came out of the river. Then the skinny cows ate the fat ones!

The king really wanted to find out the meaning of these strange dreams, but no one in his royal court was able to understand them. Then, the servant remembered Joseph, and he told the king about the man he had met in prison.

Joseph was brought from prison so the king could tell him about his dreams. Joseph immediately understood the meaning of the king's dreams and explained them. "You have been dreaming about what will happen soon. The meaning is this: First, Egypt will have seven good years with plenty of food to eat. But then there will be seven very bad years when no food will grow at all."

Joseph suggested that the king build large barns, and during the seven good years, gather all the extra food and save it. Then, when the bad years came, there would be food for the people. The king liked Joseph's plan and put him in charge of storing as much food as possible during in the good years. Joseph was now a powerful leader in Egypt.

Joseph's Brothers in Egypt

Genesis 42–45

Exactly as Joseph had explained to the king, Egypt had seven years of good crops. Then the bad years came. But it was not only in Egypt that no food grew. Crops failed all over the world, and people began to starve. Soon, people in other countries learned that there was food in Egypt.

Back in Canaan, Joseph's father and brothers were hungry because they had no food. So, old father Jacob sent his sons to Egypt to buy grain. When the brothers arrived in Egypt, they had to meet with Joseph. They did not know he was their brother who they had sold into slavery many years before.

When the brothers came before Joseph, they bowed down in deep respect. They could not recognize him since he was dressed up in his royal Egyptian clothes. Joseph recognized his brothers, but he did not reveal himself to them. He allowed them to buy as much grain as they needed.

Not long after that, the brothers had to travel to Egypt again to buy more grain. This time, Joseph asked them to bring the youngest brother, Benjamin, along on the journey.

Once again, the brothers all bowed down before Joseph. This was exactly the way Joseph had dreamed it would happen so many years earlier. And this time, Joseph could not keep back his happy tears when he saw his little brother Benjamin.

Joseph said, "I am your brother that you sold as a slave. Don't be afraid of me. You did evil to me, but God has turned it into something good. Now I have become one of the most powerful men in Egypt."

Then Joseph hugged and kissed Benjamin and his other brothers and cried tears of happiness. Joseph said to them, "Go and bring our father back here to stay with us in Egypt so we can all live as one family again."

When the king of Egypt heard that Jacob's father and brothers were coming, he gave them a wonderful piece of land in Egypt called Goshen. There, old father Jacob, his sons, and their families—who were called the Israelites—were faithful to God and lived long years with enough food for everyone.

Moses in the Basket

Exodus 1–2

Many years later, Joseph and his family had died, but their children still lived in the land of Goshen. Things did not go well for the Israelites after Joseph died, though. New kings, called pharaohs, did not like the Israelites and forced them to live as slaves in Egypt. They had to work hard and long days, and did not have much food. Yet, even in their hardship, they remained faithful to God.

The evil Pharaoh was afraid the Israelites would have so many children that they would outnumber the Egyptians and take over his kingdom. He then made a cruel and terrible decision that all the baby sons of the Israelite families must be killed. The Israelites were afraid of Pharaoh and prayed to God for help.

One Israelite mother wanted to protect her baby boy from Pharaoh's soldiers. She made a basket that could float like a boat. Then she put her baby in it and sent the basket out on the Nile River. She cried, and prayed that God would protect her little boy. She knew it would be up to God to save him.

The baby boy's sister, Miriam, hid in the weeds and watched the basket floating on the river. Then Miriam saw Pharaoh's daughter, the princess, coming down to the water for a bath. The princess saw the basket and found the baby inside. She liked the little boy and said, "I will take this baby back to the palace and raise him as my own."

"But how will I give this little baby food?" the princess wondered.

Miriam, who was still watching from her hiding place, heard this and quickly ran up to the princess. "I know an Israelite woman who can feed him," Miriam said.

The princess thanked her for the offer of help and gave the little boy back to his sister. Miriam was happy as she went home with her little brother. Their mother could take care of him as long as he was very little. And when he was big enough, he was brought to the palace where he grew up.

Moses and the Burning Bush

The princess named the baby Moses. As Moses grew older, he learned that he was an Israelite. Moses was upset that his people were living as slaves in Egypt and were treated badly, so he tried to help some of his people. But this made Pharaoh very angry. Moses had to escape from Egypt to save his own life. He went to another country, where he lived for forty years taking care of sheep.

One day, something happened to Moses that was of great importance for him and for the rest of the world. Near a mountain called Horeb, as he was watching his sheep graze, Moses suddenly saw a very strange bush on the mountain. The bush was on fire, but it did not burn up.

Moses climbed up the mountain to get a closer look at the bush. Just then, God called to him from inside the burning bush. God's voice came from the fire and said, "Don't come closer. Take off your shoes because you are standing on holy ground." Moses did what God said, but he was very afraid.

God said to Moses, "Don't be afraid, because I am with you. I have seen My people, the Israelites, suffering in Egypt and I have not forgotten them. Tell Pharaoh that the Israelites are My people and I want My people to leave Egypt. Moses, you must lead them out of Egypt."

Moses was afraid to go back to Egypt. He said to God, "Who am I to go and say this to Pharaoh? I am just a shepherd, and I cannot lead the Israelites." But God said, "I will keep you safe. Take your walking stick and use it to perform miracles in Egypt. You will lead My people to Canaan, to the land that I promised to Abraham. Go now and I will be with you." Moses was still afraid, but he obeyed God and went back to Egypt.

The Ten Plagues

Exodus 6–12

Moses went to the palace. He stood before Pharaoh and said, "God wants His people to leave Egypt."

But Pharaoh answered, "No." And he commanded that the Israelites now had to work even harder.

God then told Moses, "I will show the Pharaoh My great power. Take your walking stick and throw it to the ground." Immediately, the walking stick turned into a snake. But Pharaoh laughed and said, "I am not impressed with your God. This is something our priests are able to do as well." And the Egyptian priests came and threw down their walking sticks, and their sticks immediately turned into snakes.

Because Pharaoh did not listen to Moses, God sent ten plagues over Egypt, each one worse than the one before. First, God turned the water in Egypt into blood. The river and ponds were all filled with blood. No one could find good water to drink.

But Pharaoh still would not let God's people go.

Then, God covered the land with frogs. No one could walk without stepping on a frog. They entered into people's houses, their kitchens, and even their beds. Pharaoh called Moses and said, "I will let your people go. But first, take away the frogs." But just when God made the frogs go away, Pharaoh changed his mind and still would not let the people go.

The third plague God sent was gnats that came out of the ground. Gnats were everywhere and came in big swarms. They bit people and they bit the animals, and no one could get away from them.

Next, God sent swarms of flies over Egypt. All the houses were filled with flies. They covered everything. It was terrible for the Egyptians, and finally, Pharaoh promised Moses that the Israelites could leave if only the flies would go away. But again, just as God made the gnats and flies go away, Pharaoh broke his promise and still would not let the people leave.

Each time Moses asked Pharaoh to let the Israelites leave Egypt, the Pharaoh said no. So God said, "All of Egypt's farm animals will become sick." And so it happened. Many of the animals even died. But none of the Israelites' animals were sick. Still, the Pharaoh would not let the Israelites leave.

The sixth plague God sent was sores. Painful sores covered the Egyptian people from the top of their heads to the bottom of their feet. People were hurting too much to stand up and had to stay in bed. But the stubborn Pharaoh still would not let God's people go.

Then, God sent a terrible storm to Egypt with huge hailstones that crushed every plant and all the crops in the fields. The hail was so big that it made holes in the roofs. This hailstorm continued all day long. Finally, Pharaoh realized it was wrong to disobey God. Pharaoh said that God's people could leave Egypt. But just like before, he changed his mind as soon as God made the plague stop.

Because Pharaoh still would not let God's people leave Egypt, the Lord sent swarms of locusts all over the land. A single locust is not a problem, but when they come in swarms of millions, it is a terrible plague. The locusts ate every green plant that was still alive after the hailstorm. They ate all the fruits of the trees. Still, Pharaoh refused to let the Israelites leave Egypt.

So God covered Egypt with thick darkness. For three days it was dark, even at noon. Darkness is a nice thing at night when it's time to sleep, but it is terrible to live in darkness during the day. People could not leave home because they could not see anything.

But Pharaoh still would not let the Israelites leave Egypt.

God then said to Moses, "Pharaoh will soon let My people leave Egypt. Therefore, go and tell them to get ready to leave." Moses did as God said, and the Israelites gathered their belongings and prepared to leave Egypt. The families gathered together and ate a big meal, which is called the Passover meal.

On that same night, all the firstborn Egyptian boys began dying. Even Pharaoh's own son died. But none of the Israelite sons died.

This was the tenth plague God sent over Egypt, and it was by far the worst of them all. That night, Pharaoh called on Moses and finally said, "I have had enough. Take your people and go." The Israelites hurried to take everything they owned and they left Egypt.

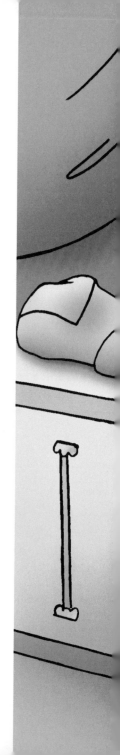

Crossing the Red Sea

122

Moses led the Israelites out of Egypt. During the day, God went ahead of His people in a thick cloud, and during the night, He went ahead of them in a pillar of fire. That way they could see that God was leading them at all times, whether it was day or night.

On their way, the Israelites came to the Red Sea, where they camped. But, once again, Pharaoh had changed his mind about letting them leave Egypt. So Pharaoh sent his army to bring the Israelites back.

The Israelites were trapped between the sea and the army. They were frightened, but Moses told them, "Don't be afraid. God will help us." God sent a strong wind that blew so hard that it pushed back the waters of the sea. A wide path opened right in front of them. The path led all the way to the other side of the sea.

The Israelites could now escape from Pharaoh's army. They took all their animals and belongings, and walked through the walls of water without even getting wet.

When Pharaoh's army reached the seashore, they also followed the path through the sea. But, just as the army marched through the middle of the sea, the wind that had been holding back the waters suddenly stopped. The water crashed back into place, and Pharaoh's whole army was washed away. God's people were safe on the other side. The Lord had saved His people from Pharaoh's army.

God's Care for the People

The Israelites were now in a large desert where they journeyed from place to place. It was hot and hard to be in the desert, and the people complained to Moses that they did not have enough to eat. So God sent food to the people in a special way. Each morning, when the people woke up, they found pieces of sweet bread, called manna, lying on the ground. In the afternoon, God sent quail into the camp that the Israelites could easily catch and eat. The people were no longer hungry.

Everywhere they went, the Israelites had enough to eat. But one day, they came to a place where there was no water to drink. The people again complained to Moses. "Give us something to drink," they said.

Moses prayed to God. And God showed him a large rock and said,
"Hit the rock with your walking stick." Moses did what God told him to.
Immediately, tasty drinking water came rushing from the rock. Now the
people could drink as much water as they wanted. Once again, God had
taken care of His people.

The Ten Commandments

Exodus 19–20

The Israelites continued their long journey in the big desert. One day, they arrived at the same mountain where Moses saw the burning bush many years before. They decided to put up their tents and camp there. When they looked up, they saw that a dark cloud covered the top of the mountain. Lightning flashed from the cloud, and loud thunder shook the earth. God was on the mountain.

Moses climbed up the mountain to talk to God. For forty days, Moses stayed on the mountaintop where God talked to him. God gave Moses laws and rules for His people to obey. God Himself carved these laws onto two large, flat stones. These laws are called the Ten Commandments. God's people live by these laws even today.

Moses carried the Ten Commandments back to the camp and read them to the Israelites. Moses told them, "We are going to build a special place to worship God. It will be a large, beautiful tent called the 'tabernacle'." They built the tabernacle in the very middle of the camp. The people made colorful curtains for it, and they decorated it with silver and gold. When the tabernacle was finished, a cloud appeared in the air just above the tabernacle. The Israelites knew that God was in the cloud!

Twelve Spies

Numbers 13–14

After many months of travel in the wilderness, the Israelites came to the edge of Canaan, the land God had promised to Abraham, Isaac, and Jacob so many years before.

    Now God said to Moses, "Send some men into the country to see what it is like." Moses picked twelve men and instructed them to go and find out if the land was a good place to live, and to see if the armies of the people there were strong.

After some time, the twelve spies returned to the camp. They said, "It is a wonderful land, but we cannot enter Canaan. The people there are giants and are mighty warriors." When the Israelite people heard these words, they were afraid.

But two of the men, Joshua and Caleb, said, "Don't be afraid. God is with us and will help us." The Israelites were still afraid and did not want to listen to them. Then God got angry with the Israelites because they would not trust Him to help them. God said, "Because you are afraid and don't trust in Me, I will not give you the land right now. Instead, you will have to stay in the desert for another forty years."

The Walls of Jericho

Joshua 1–6

Almost forty years later, the time came when God decided the Israelites would finally enter Canaan. Moses was now an old man, and he knew he would not be able to lead the people the rest of the way into the Promised Land. So Moses chose Joshua to become the new leader of the Israelite people. Joshua led the people into the land of Canaan, the land God had promised them.

137

Then, the Israelites came to the big city of Jericho. A high, thick wall surrounded the city. Joshua sent two spies into the city to look at everything. When the king of Jericho learned about the spies, he sent his soldiers to catch them, so the spies had to hide. They found a safe place to hide in a house that belonged to a woman named Rahab.

Rahab's house was built right into the city walls. Anyone inside the house could look out the windows, through the city walls, to the outside. The two Israelite spies were able to escape through those windows by climbing down a rope. They thanked Rahab for all her help, and they promised to help her later. Then, the spies went back to tell Joshua about everything they saw in Jericho.

From outside the city of Jericho, Joshua could see how thick and strong the city walls were. But he was not worried, because God had already told him how to conquer the city. Joshua commanded his army and the Israelite priests to march around the city every day for the next six days. As they marched, the soldiers of Jericho looked down at them from their safe places on top of the walls. The soldiers laughed at the Israelites and thought they were very silly.

Then, on the seventh day, God told the Israelite priests to blow their trumpets. At the same time, the people in the army shouted as loud as they could. And all at once, the city walls of Jericho tumbled down, and the Israelites easily captured the city. The two Israelite spies ran to Rahab's house. Because she had helped them escape earlier, the spies protected her and her family from harm when the Israelites took over Jericho.

Finally, after all these many years of wandering around in the desert, the Israelites had gotten their own land. God kept the promise He had made to Abraham so many years before.

Gideon and the Wet Wool

Judges 6

Like Moses, Joshua was a good leader of
the Israelite people. He knew that their lives
depended on their willingness to listen to God.
But after Joshua died, the Israelites forgot about
God. Armies from other nations came into their
land and stole their food and animals. Every time
this happened, the Israelites would remember
about God's protection. They prayed to Him for
forgiveness, and God would have mercy and help
them.

God wanted His people to call upon Him.
He sent them leaders who had great courage and
faith. These leaders were called "judges," and one
of them was Gideon.

At first, Gideon was afraid of the job God wanted him to do. Gideon said to God, "Show me that You really want me to be a leader of Your people. Give me a sign to prove it." Gideon then put a piece of wool on the ground and said to God, "Tonight, while I sleep, make this wool wet with dew. But keep the ground dry." And in the morning, when Gideon went out to see the wool, it was wet and the ground was dry. This was exactly as Gideon had asked it to be.

Gideon was still afraid, so the next night he put the wool out again. This time, he said to God, "Lord, I am very sorry, but I need another sign from You. In the morning, let the wool be dry but cover the ground with dew." When he woke up the next morning, the wool was dry, but everywhere else the ground was wet with dew. Now Gideon knew for sure that God wanted him to be a leader and judge in Israel.

Gideon's Three Hundred Men

Gideon prepared for war against the Midianites. He gathered as many soldiers as he could, because he wanted to be sure to defeat the mighty Midianite army. Many thousands of men came to be in Gideon's army. But God told Gideon that the army was too big and he would have to send most of them back home. Gideon ended up with a small army of only three hundred men. But God assured Gideon that it was enough to win the battle.

God had a very smart plan for how only three hundred Israelites would defeat the large army of the Midianites. God explained to Gideon that each soldier must carry a torch, a clay pot, and a horn. Gideon instructed his men to light their torches, but to cover them with the clay pots to hide the light. In this way, they could sneak into the Midianites' camp without being seen.

Gideon had the men stand on the hilltops around the Midianite camp. Then, on Gideon's signal, every man smashed his clay pot and blew his horn. The loud noise woke the Midianites from their sleep. When they heard the loud noise of the trumpets blowing and saw the lights on the hill tops, it looked and sounded like they were surrounded by a large army. They thought there was no escape.

The Midianites ran out of their tents to try to get away. But in the darkness, they ran into one another. This made them think their enemy was in their camp, so they started fighting one another in the darkness. The Midianites destroyed themselves. In this way, God gave Gideon and his three hundred men a great victory over a much larger army.

Samson the Super Strong

Judges 13

Years later, after Gideon died, God sent a new judge and leader to Israel. His name was Samson. God told Samson that he must never cut his hair. God said, "If you do not cut your hair, I will make you stronger than any other man on earth." Samson obeyed God. His hair grew until it was very long and his beard grew until it was big and flowing.

Even as a young man, Samson was super strong, just as God said he would be. Once, Samson was attacked by a big, strong lion, but Samson was so strong that he easily killed the lion with his bare hands.

The people of Israel had many disagreements with their neighbors, especially the Philistines. One night, Samson was in a city called Gaza. The city was surrounded by a tall, thick wall and had big, heavy gates for protection. When the Philistines found out that Samson was in the city, they decided to try to catch him. So they blocked the gates from the outside to trap Samson inside the city walls. But Samson easily tore the gates off of the walls, put them on his back, and carried them away. The Philistines were shocked at how strong Samson was.

A beautiful woman named Delilah lived in Gaza, and Samson fell in love with her. The Philistines threatened Delilah. They made her find out the secret of Samson's strength. Delilah was afraid of the Philistines, so she begged Samson to tell her his secret. Two times she asked, and Samson would not tell her. But the third time she asked him to tell her the secret of his strength, Delilah cried. Samson felt sorry for her, and he said, "If my hair is cut off, I will lose my strength and become as weak as any man." So while he was sleeping, Delilah had Samson's hair cut off. Immediately, Samson's strength left him.

Now that Samson's strength was gone, his enemies, the Philistines, could easily catch him. They tied him up and threw him in prison. They were afraid he would escape, so they blinded him too. In prison, Samson was forced to work very hard by pushing a big, heavy stone to grind grain.

One day, the Philistines held a big party to worship their god, Dagon. More than three thousand people were at the party. As they drank, they had the wicked idea of making fun of Samson, so they brought him up from the prison. As the guards chained him between the pillars of the building, people laughed and spat at blind Samson. He had been in prison long enough that much of his hair had grown back. As the Philistines continued their party, Samson prayed his last prayer to God. He said, "God, please give me back my strength just this one more time." God made him strong again.

Samson pushed as hard as he could. The pillars fell and the roof came crashing down on the wicked Philistines. No one in the big building escaped.

Samuel, The Boy Who Listened to God

1 Samuel 1–3

Israel's next great leader was Samuel. But years before Samuel was born, when his mother, Hannah, had no children, she prayed to God that she would have a baby. Years passed, and one day Hannah made a promise to God. "If I have a son," she said, "he will be Your special servant all of his life." God answered Hannah's prayer, and Samuel was born.

When Samuel was still a very young boy, Hannah kept her promise to God. She took Samuel to a priest named Eli. She told Eli, "I want Samuel to grow up working in the temple with you. It is a promise I made to God before Samuel was born, and now I want to keep my promise." Then Eli began to take care of Samuel.

Hannah visited Samuel in the temple every year, and every year she brought him a new coat. Eli, the priest, loved Samuel dearly and treated him like he was his own son. Eli told Samuel all about God, and he also taught him everything about being a servant in God's temple.

Years went by, and Samuel was now about thirteen years old. One night, while he was sleeping in the temple, Samuel heard a voice. The voice was calling his name. "Samuel! Samuel!"

Samuel thought it was Eli calling to him from his room. He ran to Eli. "Did you call me?" Samuel asked. But Eli had not called him, so Samuel went back to bed.

Then the voice called a second time. "Samuel! Samuel!" Once more Samuel ran to Eli. And again Eli said, "I did not call you. Go back to bed." Samuel heard the voice a third time, and again he went to Eli. Now Eli realized it was not just something Samuel was dreaming. Eli said, "I think God is speaking to you. The next time you hear the voice, say, 'Speak, Lord. I am your servant and I am listening.' "

Samuel went back to bed. A little later, he heard the voice again. This time, Samuel said, "Speak, Lord. I am Your servant. I am ready to listen." From that night on, God often spoke to young Samuel. When people learned that Samuel talked with God, they came to him for advice. He became a prophet when he was still just a boy because God spoke to him about things that were to happen. Later, when Samuel was a young man, he became the leader of the Israelite people.

David and Goliath

1 Samuel 17

Samuel was the leader in Israel for many years, and he taught people to follow God. But as he grew older, the Israelites demanded to have a new leader. They wanted the kind of king many other nations had. So the people demanded that Samuel find someone to be king and to lead Israel.

Samuel found the king God had chosen for the people of Israel. He was an impressive man named Saul. He was taller than everyone else, and he was a strong warrior. The people of Israel believed that Saul would be a great king for them. They especially wanted him to defeat their worst enemy, the Philistines.

In the army of the Philistines was a giant named Goliath, who was more than nine feet tall. Goliath was mean. He made fun of the Israelites, and he made fun of God. Every day, Goliath stood near Saul's army and dared someone to fight him. "Come and fight me, if you are brave enough," Goliath shouted. But all of Israel's soldiers were afraid of him because he was so big and strong and mean. And no one was willing to fight him.

Then, one day, a young boy named David came to the Israelite camp to visit his brothers, who were soldiers in the army. David was a shepherd (in Israel, it was a normal thing for boys to take care of the family's sheep).

As he visited with his brothers, David could see how all the soldiers in the Israelite army were afraid of Goliath. But David was not afraid.

David went to King Saul and said, "I am not afraid of Goliath. I will fight him."

But Saul said, "You are just a little boy. How can you defeat the giant?"

David replied, "With God's help. I have killed lions and bears who tried to steal my sheep. God will also help me fight Goliath."

When Saul heard these brave words, he gave David his own sword and dressed him with his helmet and armor. But the helmet and armor were much too heavy for little David to wear, so he gave them back to Saul.

Instead, David chose five smooth stones from the ground. He put one stone in his sling. Then he went right up to Goliath and shouted, "You fight me with your sword, your spear, and all your strength. But I will fight with the strength God will give me." David ran toward Goliath, swinging the sling around and around.

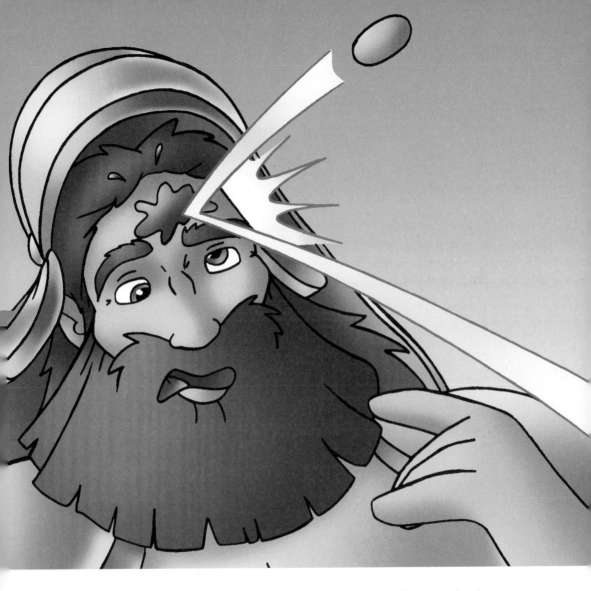

David let the stone fly, and it hit Goliath right above his eyes in the forehead! The giant fell down to the ground. David ran up to him, grabbed Goliath's own sword, and cut off his head. The wicked Goliath was defeated.

The Philistines never expected their army to be defeated, especially by a little boy. They were so surprised that all the Philistine soldiers ran away. But everyone in Israel was excited, and they celebrated that God had made it possible for a shepherd boy to defeat the mighty giant. David became a famous hero in Israel.

Saul and David

Years later, when David was a man, he became a leader in the Israelite army. He won many battles, and people said, "David is a greater warrior than Saul." These words made King Saul very jealous. Secretly he began looking for ways to kill David. One day, while they had dinner together, Saul threw his spear at David.

The spear missed, but David had to run for his life. David and his
friend Jonathan ran all the way to the mountains. Saul and his soldiers
followed David because the angry king wanted to find him and kill him.

David and his friends hid inside a cave. Saul had followed, but he did not see where David and his friends went. Saul and his men camped for the night at the entrance of the same cave where David was hiding. While they were asleep, David and his men went out of the cave and snuck up on them.

Saul had fallen into a deep sleep, with his spear right beside him. David's men said, "Look! Here is your chance to kill Saul and take over." But David did not want to kill Saul. He said, "God made Saul king. It would be wrong to kill him." Instead, David cut off a piece of Saul's coat and snuck away without waking up anyone.

Early the next morning, David stood on top of a hill and called out to Saul. He held up the piece of Saul's coat he had cut off and said, "Do you see that I could have killed you last night if I wanted to? But I did not harm you at all. You have nothing to fear from me. So why are you trying to kill me?" And Saul said, "You are right, David. You have been kind to me and spared my life." Saul and his soldiers went back home. But in his heart, Saul still hated David.

When Saul died, people made David their new king. David was a great king. He built a great kingdom and defeated Israel's many enemies. He captured the city of Jerusalem and built his big palace there. David was a good king because he listened to God and tried to obey Him. David was skilled with many things. He was a great warrior, but also a great poet and musician. David played the harp and wrote many songs, called *psalms*, about God's love and about trusting God during difficult times.

Solomon, The Wise King

1 Kings 2–10

After David died, his son, Solomon, became king. Solomon prayed to God to give him wisdom so he could be a good king and rule wisely. Solomon was so wise that people from many other countries heard of his wisdom. People from faraway places came to meet him and listen to him.

God also made Solomon very rich. He had more wealth than any other king who ever ruled in Israel. Solomon used his wealth to build the first temple in Jerusalem. This temple was very special because God told Solomon how to build it, and because inside the temple was the box that held the Ten Commandments.

The temple was very expensive to build. Everything in it was covered with gold and silver and sparkling jewels. When the temple was finished, there was a big party that lasted for seven days. During this party, Solomon dedicated the temple to God. And God dwelled in the temple that Solomon built. These were truly blessed times for Israel.

Elijah, Prophet of Fire

1 Kings 17

After King Solomon lived and died, there were many very bad kings in Israel. These kings did not care about God at all. Instead, they prayed to idols made of rock and wood. One of the worst kings was Ahab. He decided that everybody should worship an idol named Baal.

Almost everyone obeyed Ahab because he was the king. Ahab said that anyone who worshiped God would be killed. But there were seven thousand people in Israel who still believed in the true God. One of them was a prophet named Elijah. God told Elijah to go and tell King Ahab that all the people should begin to obey God and stop worshiping Baal. But Ahab did not want to listen to Elijah, and that made God very angry.

So God punished King Ahab and Israel by not letting rain fall in Israel for a very long time. It was difficult to find anything to eat, because without rain, no plants would grow. King Ahab wanted to kill Elijah. Since Elijah was God's prophet, Ahab blamed him for the lack of rain. But Elijah was safe, far away from King Ahab. He was hiding in a place where no one else lived.

Although everything in the land was now completely dried out because no rain had fallen for months, Elijah was living well beside a little stream that still had water. Every morning, black birds brought pieces of bread and meat to Elijah, and he had more than enough food to eat. This is how God kept Elijah alive while he was hiding from the evil king's soldiers.

The Big Test

Three years went by, but King Ahab continued to be stubborn and wicked; he would not follow God. Instead, Ahab built more and more idols to Baal. Again, God sent Elijah to talk to Ahab. Elijah asked, "Why do you still worship the false god Baal? Let us have a contest between the true living God and your Baal, who is no god at all. This will prove once and for all which God is real."

King Ahab agreed to the contest. He gathered all the leaders of Israel on a high mountain. He also gathered hundreds of priests who also believed in Baal. Then they built two altars, one for God and one for Baal. They placed wood on the altars.

Elijah said to the king's priests, "Don't light the wood on fire. Instead, pray to your god, Baal. If he is real, he can light the fire on the altar. I will pray to the living God to send fire from heaven and burn the wood on the altar built for Him. Let us agree that from this day on we will believe in whichever god sends fire from the heavens."

Hundreds of the king's priests begged Baal to light a fire on the altar. But nothing happened. Elijah teased the priests and shouted to them, "Maybe Baal cannot hear you. You should shout louder. Or maybe Baal is busy or asleep." So the king's priests yelled louder and louder, and danced around the altar more wildly, but absolutely nothing happened.

After several hours, Ahab's priests had to give up and admit that Baal was not real. Now it was Elijah's turn. He surprised the king's people by commanding that water be poured all over the altar. He had so much water poured on everything that the wood and the altar were completely wet. Elijah also dug a ditch around the altar and it filled up with water.

Everybody watched as Elijah raised his hands and quietly prayed to God. He said, "Dear Lord, show everyone here that You are the one and only true God, that I am Your servant, and that people must never again forget about You." After Elijah prayed, a huge flame came down from the sky and hit the altar with a loud noise. The flame burned everything on the altar. Even the stones the altar was built of burned, and all the water around the altar disappeared as well. The king's people could hardly believe what they saw, and they all fell to their knees and shouted, "God is the true God."

The Chariot of Fire

Many years went by, and Elijah grew older and older. It was time for someone to replace him as God's prophet. One day, God led Elijah to a man named Elisha. Like Elijah, Elisha also loved God, listened to Him, and obeyed Him. The two men became very close friends. Elisha thought that Elijah was the best person he had ever met.

One day, Elijah took Elisha out on a very long walk. Elisha knew the day had come for Elijah to leave this world. He was very sad about this and wanted to follow Elijah wherever he went. When they reached the Jordan River, Elijah took off his cloak and hit the water with it. Suddenly, the water in the river pulled back and Elijah and Elisha walked across on dry land.

When they had crossed to the other side of the river, Elijah said, "I am about to leave you. Before I go, I want to give you something. What do you want?" Elisha replied, "I want to have the kind of power you have." "It is much to wish for," said Elijah. "I will be leaving soon. But if God lets you see me leave, that means He will give you what you want."

They continued walking. Then, all at once, Elisha saw a chariot of fire pulled by fiery horses coming from the heavens. As it came between them, Elijah got into the chariot. Then, a giant whirlwind lifted Elijah and the chariot up into the air and carried him higher and higher, until Elisha could not see him anymore.

Elisha saw that Elijah's cloak lay on the ground. He picked it up and walked back to the river. When he came to the river, he took Elijah's cloak in his hands and hit the water with it, just as Elijah had done. Once more, the water pulled back so he could cross on dry ground. Now Elisha knew that God had given him the same powers that Elijah had. From that day on, Elisha was a very trusted and important prophet in Israel, just like Elijah.

Daniel's Friends in the Burning Fire

Daniel 3

The Israelites were slaves when they lived in Egypt, then Moses led them to the Promised Land where they had freedom. Now, hundreds of years later, the Israelites were again living as slaves. Israel's many bad and evil kings had forgotten all about God, so God allowed the king of Babylon and his armies to destroy Jerusalem. When that happened, thousands of Israelites were captured and taken to Babylon to live as slaves.

Babylon's King Nebuchadnezzar had built a huge idol. He had the idol covered with gold, and placed it right in the middle of the city. Then, he commanded everyone to bow down and worship the idol.

But three Israelite friends named Shadrach, Meshach, and Abednego did not worship the idol. They were faithful to God and would worship only Him.

The king became very angry and told them, "If you do not worship my idol, I will throw you into the fire in the big furnace." The men said, "God can save us from the fire. But even if He does not save us, we will not worship the idol. No matter what happens, we will worship only the one true God."

The king turned to his soldiers and said, "Put more wood in the furnace
to make the fire as hot as you can." The soldiers did as the king said.
Never before had the furnace burned so hot. Then they threw the three
men right into the fire while the king watched.

But an amazing thing happened. The fire did not hurt the Israelite men at all! It did not even burn their clothes. Then, as they walked around inside the furnace, it looked like there were now four people. King Nebuchadnezzar was horrified when he saw this. He said, "I put three people in the fire. But now I see four men in the furnace, and one of them looks like a son of the gods."

The king called the three men out of the furnace, and they calmly walked out. They did not even smell burned from the fire they had been in. King Nebuchadnezzar knew now that God had saved them, so he made a new law in Babylon. Now Nebuchadnezzar demanded that no one should ever say anything bad about the God of Israel. The three friends had trusted in God, and He saved them. The people everywhere in Babylon came to know what God had done on this day.

Daniel and the Lions

Daniel 6

Daniel was wise and honest in everything he did, and although he was a slave, he worked closely with the kings in Babylon. The kings liked Daniel very much. But other men who also worked in the palace did not like Daniel. They were jealous that the kings trusted him, an Israelite slave, with so much. So they decided to set a trap for Daniel.

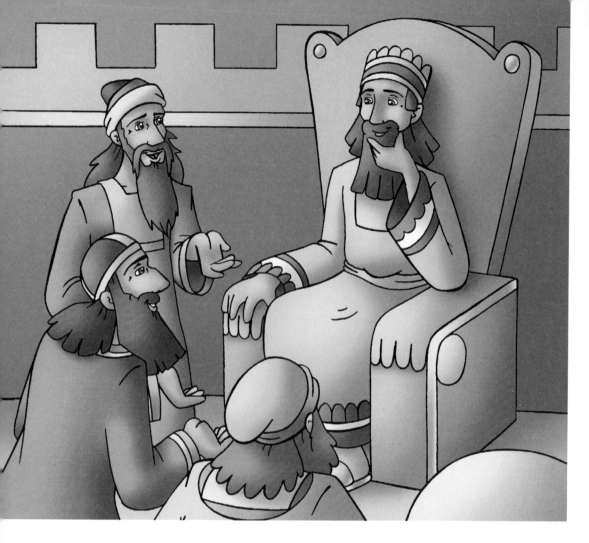

These wicked men knew Daniel prayed to God three times every day. So they went to the king and said, "Why don't you make a new law that for the next thirty days, people pray only to you and no one else? This will show that they are loyal to you." The king liked this idea so much that he also decided that anyone who did not pray to him would be thrown into a lion's den.

But Daniel was a faithful man, and he did not stop praying to God. It was easy for the wicked men to catch him breaking this law. The men tattled to the king that Daniel was praying to God and not to the king; now Daniel had to be thrown to the lions. The king was very sad because he liked Daniel so much. But at the same time, he knew that because he was the king and he had made the law himself, he could not break it.

Soldiers came and arrested Daniel. They took him to a pit filled with hungry lions. Then the soldiers threw him down into the pit. The wicked men were happy to finally get rid of Daniel.

But the king was upset and could not sleep. He stayed awake all night. He did not drink or eat anything. He was thinking all the time about the terrible lions and poor Daniel.

Early the next morning, as soon as the first light came, the king rushed to the pit where Daniel and lions were. Although he did not expect an answer, he called, "Daniel! Daniel! Are you there?"

What a surprise when Daniel replied, "Yes, king, I am alive and well. God sent an angel and it stopped the lions from hurting me. God kept me safe." The king was very happy and ordered Daniel to be pulled up from the pit. Then he sent out a message to the whole kingdom of Babylon, so everyone would know how God had saved Daniel from the lions. And God once more showed people in Babylon that He is the one true God that must be worshiped and obeyed.

Queen Esther

King Xerxes ruled over the mighty empire of Persia. When he decided it was time to find a wife, his servants searched the land for the most beautiful woman they could find. An Israelite woman named Esther was brought before King Xerxes, and when he saw her, he was very pleased. He was so pleased, he set the royal crown on her head and Esther became the queen!

Esther's uncle, Mordecai, had adopted her when she was a child. One day, as he sat by the palace gates, Mordecai overheard some men plotting to kill the king. Mordecai immediately went to Queen Esther and warned her so she could tell this to the king. The bad men were then arrested, and the king was very grateful to Mordecai for his help.

Sometime later, a powerful man named Haman became very angry at Mordecai. Haman knew that Mordecai was an Israelite and not a Persian, so to get back at Mordecai, he tricked the king into passing a law that made it all right to kill Israelites. King Xerxes went along with this terrible law, but he did not know that his beloved Queen Esther was also an Israelite.

Esther was very afraid for herself and her people, the Israelites. But she was also brave, and she went to visit the king. She wanted to ask him to change the law that Haman had tricked him into making. When the king saw her, he said, "What can I do for you, dear Queen? I will give you whatever you ask, up to half my kingdom."

Esther answered, "My king, Haman has promised a reward to anyone who kills my people, the Israelites. If you really care for me and are willing to help, you can save my people and me; that is what I really want."

Now, the king got very angry. He realized how Haman had convinced him to make such a bad law. So, the king changed the law and ordered Haman to be hanged instead. And Esther became famous as the person who saved herself, Mordecai, and all of the Israelite people.

Jonah and the Whale

The Book of Jonah

There was a man named Jonah, and there was a city called Nineveh. Nineveh was one of the biggest cities in the world, but it was also one of the most terrible places. The people there were wicked and did terrible things to one another. This made God very sad and angry. He said to Jonah, "Go and warn the people in this city that if they don't stop their evil actions, I will destroy their city."

But Jonah did not want to go to Nineveh. He was afraid of what the people would do to him if he gave them this message from God. Instead, he went to the harbor, where all the big ships were, to get on a boat that was going far away. He just made it there as one of the boats was about to leave the harbor to sail across the sea, far, far away.

Jonah went down below deck to take a nap. He wanted to forget that he was running away from the job God had asked him to do. As the boat was moving smoothly through the waters, Jonah fell asleep.

While he was asleep, God caused a terrible storm to rise over the sea. Although the sailors on this boat were used to sailing through big storms and tall waves, this storm terrified them. The sailors woke Jonah up from his deep sleep. Jonah could see how afraid they were. Immediately, Jonah knew the storm was sent by God and why.

Jonah said to the sailors, "I should never have been on board this ship. It is my fault, because I should have gone to Nineveh. Instead, I was trying to run away from God by sailing in the opposite direction. Now you must throw me into the sea. Then God will make the storm go away."

So the sailors threw Jonah into the sea. Immediately, the wind stopped blowing and the waves became flat. The dark gray sky turned to blue, and the sun started to shine again. Everything was nice and quiet, and the men on the ship were safe.

But Jonah was sinking under the water. He went deeper and deeper and deeper into the sea. He saw a big shadow approaching right under him from the depths of the sea. It came closer and closer.

The shadow was a big whale that came and swallowed Jonah right up. It swallowed him in one mouthful. Jonah went all the way down through the belly of the whale.

It was dark and smelled terrible inside the belly of the whale. Everything it ate was swallowed down into its belly, along with Jonah. Although it was a scary and dark place to be, inside the belly of the whale, deep down in the sea, Jonah knew that God could still hear him. So he started to pray to God. Jonah prayed for three days and nights.

God had not forgotten Jonah. All the time as Jonah was praying to God, the whale was swimming toward land. On the third day, it spit Jonah up on the seashore. Jonah thanked God and said, "From now on I will always obey what You tell me to do."

Once again, God told Jonah, "Go to Nineveh and warn the people of what I will do." This time, Jonah obeyed God and went to Nineveh. He warned the people there that if they did not stop their evil actions, God would destroy them and their city. The people listened to Jonah and agreed that their lives had been evil. They also asked God to forgive them. God forgave the people in Nineveh, saved their lives, and did not destroy their city.

The New Testament

Mary and Gabriel

More than two thousand years ago, there was a young woman named Mary. God used her in a very special way. Mary lived in Israel in a small town called Nazareth, and she was planning to marry a man named Joseph.

One day, God's angel Gabriel appeared and stood before Mary. He was in a very bright light that almost looked like fire. Gabriel said, "Mary, you are the most blessed of all women. Do not be afraid. God has sent me to tell you that God is bringing His Son into the world, and you will give birth to His Son. You shall name the boy Jesus."

Mary did not understand what the angel had just told her. She asked, "How can this happen? I am not married, so how could I give birth to a child?" The angel answered, "God's power will come over you. And your child will be called the holy Son of God. Nothing is impossible for God." Mary was happy to be chosen by God for this. But she was also worried about Joseph. Would he believe what Gabriel had said?

God took care of everything. One night, an angel spoke to Joseph in a dream. The angel told him that Mary would have a son by the Holy Spirit. The angel also told Joseph he must marry her and be the father of her child. So Joseph obeyed God and married Mary soon after.

Jesus Is Born in Bethlehem

Luke 2

It was time for the baby to be born. But Mary and Joseph had to travel to the town of Bethlehem, many miles away from their home in Nazareth. This journey was by order of the Roman emperor. He wanted to know how many people lived in his kingdom so he could collect taxes from them. It was a long and hard journey to travel to Bethlehem, especially for Mary.

When Joseph and Mary arrived in Bethlehem, they were tired and hungry. Joseph looked for a place to stay, but he could not find one. No one in the town had a room for them to stay in. Instead, Mary and Joseph stayed in a stable, where people kept their animals. It was cold and dark inside the stable, but God wanted them to be exactly right there in that humble place.

It was a dark night in Bethlehem when Jesus was born. He was just as little and helpless as any newborn baby. Mary hugged baby Jesus and wrapped Him in a cloth and laid Him in a manger. God's own Son, the Savior God promised long ago, had been born. At that moment, only Mary and Joseph knew that the Son of God was born that night in Bethlehem.

That same night, in the fields near Bethlehem, shepherds were guarding their sheep. Suddenly, the shepherds saw a bright light in the sky. In the air above them, angels were everywhere and were singing wonderful things about what God had done that night in Bethlehem. "Praise God in heaven. Peace on earth to everyone who pleases God," the angels sang.

The angels told the shepherds, "A special child has been born tonight in Bethlehem. You will find Him in a stable, wrapped in a cloth and laid in a manger. Glory to God!"

What wonderful news this was! After the angels left and went back to heaven, the shepherds hurried to Bethlehem where they found Mary, Joseph, and the little baby. When they saw Jesus, the shepherds knew in their hearts that the angels had told them the truth. He was God's own Son. They praised God for the child. And they told Mary everything the angels had told them out in the fields. Mary thought about all this and wondered what it all meant.

The Wise Men

Matthew 2

Far away, in another country, there lived some very wise men. They had read many books, and they studied the stars at night. One night, they saw a new star in the sky that they had never seen before. The men said to one another, "This new star is a sign that a King has been born in Judah. Come, let us go to Israel to find the new King."

The Wise Men took their camels and prepared gifts for the King, and they began their long journey to the West, toward Israel. After many months, they arrived in Jerusalem. They went to the palace of King Herod and said, "We know that a new King has been born in Israel because we have seen His star. We have come to kneel down before Him and give Him our gifts."

But the evil King Herod answered them, "I don't know where this newborn King is. But when you find Him, let me know so I also can go and honor Him." But Herod was lying. He did not want to honor the new King. He wanted to kill Him because Herod was very jealous and wicked.

The Wise Men didn't know that Herod was lying, so they agreed to return and tell him where he could find the new King. Then they continued their search. The star showed them the way to Bethlehem, to the very place where Jesus was. They kneeled down and worshiped Jesus and gave Him their fine and expensive gifts. They were the kind of gifts people then would give to a king: gold, frankincense, and myrrh.

That same night, as the Wise Men slept, an angel came to them in a dream. The angel told them they should not go back to tell King Herod where they had found Jesus. So the Wise Men went back home a different way.

When the Wise Men did not come back to the palace in Jerusalem, King Herod was angry. He told his soldiers, "Go to Bethlehem and kill every baby boy you find in the town."

But the soldiers did not find Jesus in Bethlehem. Joseph had also been warned in a dream by God's angel about what Herod planned to do. The angel said, "Joseph, get up and take your family to Egypt. You will be safe there from Herod." That very night, Joseph took Mary and Jesus and went to Egypt. They stayed in Egypt until King Herod died. Then they went back to Israel to live in Nazareth. And that is where Jesus grew up.

Jesus in the Temple

Luke 2:41–51

When Jesus was twelve years old, Mary and Joseph took Him on a long journey to Jerusalem. Each year, many people went to Jerusalem for the Passover celebration. There would be big crowds everywhere in the city. What a wonderful journey to Jerusalem it was!

When they came to Jerusalem, they went into the temple where the Passover celebration was held. They prayed to God and sang many songs to praise Him. Jesus loved to be in the temple with His family and friends. The celebration lasted seven days, and then people began to travel back to their homes. Joseph and Mary also started back to their home in Nazareth with a large group of their family and friends.

Mary and Joseph did not see Jesus when they left Jerusalem, but they were sure He was traveling ahead of them with some of their relatives. They thought they would catch up with Him along the way, so as they walked, they looked for him. But the first night of their journey passed and they did not see Jesus. They became very worried when they realized Jesus was missing. Mary and Joseph rushed back to Jerusalem to find Him.

When they came to Jerusalem, they went right into the temple. And to their relief, Mary and Joseph saw Jesus as He was sitting with the priests who served in the temple. Jesus was listening to them, and asking them many questions. The priests were astonished to meet and listen to such a wise boy. It was very clear to them that Jesus, who was only twelve years old, knew much about God, and they wondered how this could be.

Mary said to Jesus, "Son! We have been so worried about You and have looked for You everywhere! Why did You stay behind instead of coming home with us?"

Jesus said, "Why were you looking for Me? Didn't you know that I belong here in My Father's house?" Jesus said this because He knew He was the Son of God. Mary immediately realized that Jesus was right. Then Jesus went home to Nazareth with Mary and Joseph, and He lived there until He was a young man.

John the Baptist

Mark 1:1–12

A man called "John the Baptizer" lived far from town, near the Jordan River. His clothes were made from camel hair, and he wore a wide leather belt. He caught locusts and ate them with wild honey. John preached to anyone who would listen. "Turn away from your sinful ways toward God," John said. "Be baptized, for God is about to do something wonderful very soon. You must get ready. God's messenger will soon be here!"

John baptized many people in the Jordan River. This Baptism meant that people wanted to repent from their sins and receive forgiveness. John stood in the Jordan River every day and baptized many people who wanted forgiveness.

One day, Jesus came to the Jordan River where John was baptizing
people. Jesus knew John because they were cousins. He asked to be
baptized by him, but John said, "Jesus, You don't need to be baptized.
It is I who needs to be baptized by You." But Jesus insisted, "I want you
to baptize Me, John. This is how it must be." So John baptized Jesus.

When Jesus came up from the water after His Baptism, something fantastic happened. The heavens opened, and the voice of God could be heard coming from high in the sky. God said, "This is My Son. I am very pleased with Him." And then it looked as if a white dove was descending from heaven upon Jesus. This was God's Holy Spirit.

John told all of the people there, "Jesus is God's great messenger. This is the One I have been telling you about."

"Come and Follow Me"

Mark 1:16–20

After Jesus was baptized, He began teaching people about God and His kingdom.

One day, as Jesus was walking by the shore of the Sea of Galilee, He saw some men in fishing boats. The fishermen had big nets that they used to catch fish.

These men's names were Peter, Andrew, John, and James. Jesus called out to them and said, "Come and follow Me. I will teach you how to fish for men." Immediately, the men left their boats and nets and followed Jesus. Now Jesus had four new friends. They were called "disciples." They traveled with Jesus, listened to everything He taught, and saw everything He did. One day, they would teach His message to others.

Jesus made other friends, and He called them to follow Him too. Soon, Jesus had twelve disciples who followed wherever Jesus went. For the next three years, they traveled all over Israel, teaching people about God and His kingdom, healing them, and forgiving their sins.

The Wedding at Cana

John 2:1–11

Jesus and some of His disciples were invited to a big wedding in Cana. Jesus' mother, Mary, was also invited. It was a very big party where the most wonderful food and wine were served, and there was music and singing. Everyone was happy, and celebrated with the young couple that had just been married.

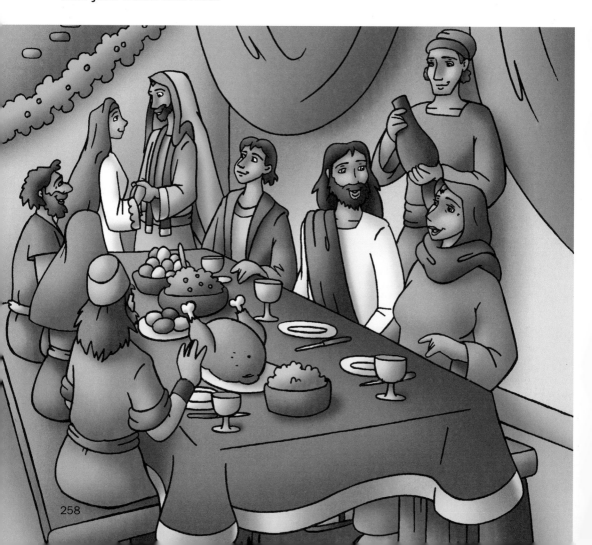

But during the party, Mary came to Jesus and told Him some bad news. "The wine has run out, and they have no more to serve to the wedding guests," she said. Jesus said to her, "What do you want Me to do? My time has not yet come." Then Mary went to the servants and told them to do whatever Jesus said to do.

There were six big, empty jars in the kitchen. Jesus pointed at the jars and said to the servants, "Fill these empty jars with water." They did what Jesus said and filled them with water.

"Now, take some and serve it to the master," Jesus said.

Again, the servants did what Jesus said. They took water from the jars and served it to the master. But it was no longer water. Jesus had turned it into wine! Everyone said it was the best wine they had ever tasted. Because Jesus was God the Son, He had the power to do this. And it was only the first of many miracles Jesus was going to do.

"Don't Worry about Tomorrow"

Matthew 6:25–34

Now everyone was talking about Jesus. The people loved to hear what He taught about God, and every day, more and more people followed Him. But they wondered who Jesus was, and how He could teach with so much wisdom.

One day, Jesus and His disciples were on the side of a mountain. Jesus was teaching them about the kingdom of God. A crowd of people had also followed, and they gathered close by and listened too.

Jesus said, "Look at the birds. Do they build barns to store their food for the future? No, but God still feeds them. Don't be afraid that you might not have food. Don't be afraid that you might not have clothes. God will take care of you. Ask God for food and ask Him for the things you need to live. But don't worry about tomorrow. Just ask God for the things you need today."

Next, Jesus told them, "Look at the flowers. They don't worry about what they wear. Yet God dresses them in the most beautiful colors. To God, you are more important than all the birds. And you are more important than all the flowers on earth. Yet God takes care of the flowers and the birds, so He will also take even better care of you, always!"

Through the Roof to Jesus

Mark 2:1–12

In every town Jesus entered, He healed people of their illness and forgave their sin. He gave blind people their sight, He gave deaf people their hearing, and He made lame people walk. And everywhere He went, Jesus taught people about God.

One day, He was teaching in a house in Capernaum. The house was so crowded with people that no one else could get inside.

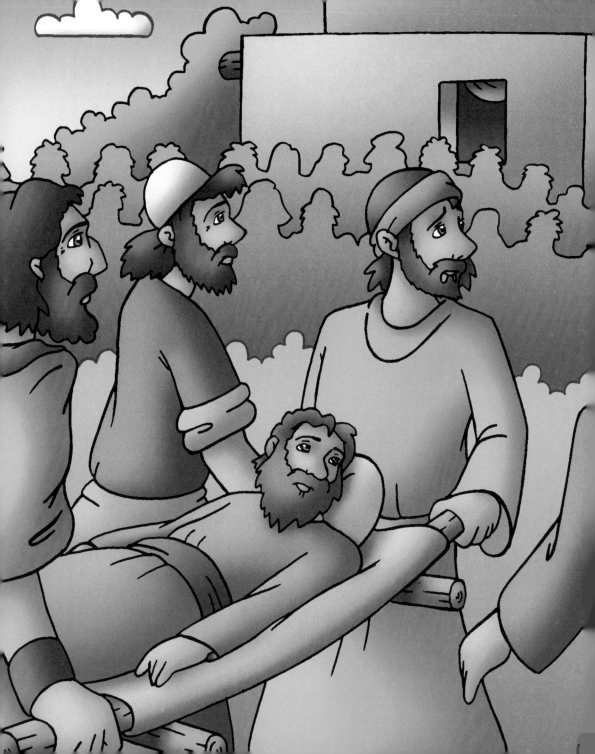

Four men came to the house where Jesus was. They took with them a friend who lay on a stretcher because he could not walk. These men knew that Jesus could make their friend walk again. They tried to take their friend inside, but they could not enter the house because it was too crowded. But they wanted to bring their friend to Jesus, so they didn't give up.

Then the men had a smart idea. They climbed up on the roof of the house and carried their friend with them. They made a hole in the roof so they could lower their friend down into the room right in front of Jesus. Everybody looked at the man who was lying on the stretcher.

Jesus was happy to see that the men did so much to bring their friend to Him. He looked at the man and said, "Your sins are forgiven." But the people in the house got angry and said, "Only God can forgive sins." Jesus replied, "You don't believe that I have the power to forgive sins, do you? Well, do you think I have the power to make this man walk?"

Then Jesus said to the man, "Stand up! Pick up your stretcher and go home." Immediately, the man jumped up. He picked up his stretcher and walked right through the crowd. The people who saw this were amazed. They said, "We have never seen anything like this before."

Two Fish and Five Loaves of Bread

John 6:1–14

On another day, Jesus and His disciples went up in the mountains to spend some time alone. They were far away from town, but people had seen Jesus leave and followed Him. People kept coming until there were more than five thousand who wanted to hear Jesus teach and to have Him heal their diseases. It was now getting late, and everyone was very hungry.

The disciples said, "Jesus, ask the people to leave now so they can go home and get something to eat." But they were very far from the town, and Jesus knew it would take the hungry people many hours to get back home. Jesus said to the disciples, "Give these people some food." But the disciples said, "We have no food, and we have no money to buy food for them."

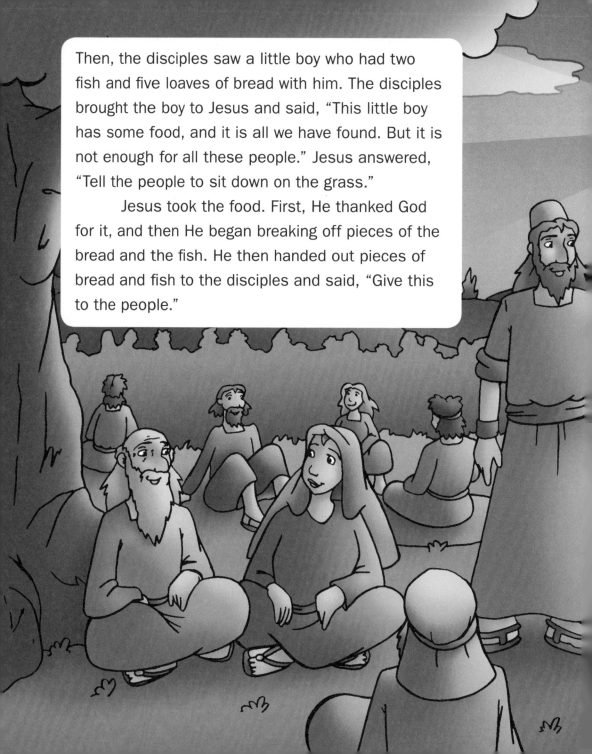

Then, the disciples saw a little boy who had two fish and five loaves of bread with him. The disciples brought the boy to Jesus and said, "This little boy has some food, and it is all we have found. But it is not enough for all these people." Jesus answered, "Tell the people to sit down on the grass."

Jesus took the food. First, He thanked God for it, and then He began breaking off pieces of the bread and the fish. He then handed out pieces of bread and fish to the disciples and said, "Give this to the people."

The disciples passed out bread and fish to everyone who was there. All the people ate until they were full. Then the disciples gathered the food that was left. There were twelve baskets full of leftovers! In Jesus' hands, the little boy's five loaves of bread and two fish fed more than five thousand people on that day. It was a miracle!

Jesus Walks on Water

Matthew 14:22–32

Jesus told His disciples that He wanted to go up on a mountain by Himself. He wanted to spend time praying to God, and He would meet them afterward. So Jesus told the disciples to take a boat and sail across the big lake of Gennesaret. He would meet them on the other side of the lake when He was done praying.

Jesus went up to pray, and the disciples set sail in a boat. After they sailed far out on the big lake, a very strong storm with dark, rainy skies suddenly came upon the boat. Big waves crashed against the boat again and again, and the disciples were very frightened. They were afraid their boat would sink.

Just as it looked like all was lost, Jesus came walking on the water to meet them. In His white clothes, Jesus looked like a ghost to the disciples, and they were even more afraid. But then Jesus called to them, "Don't be afraid. It is Me." Peter wanted to be sure it was Jesus so he called out, "Jesus, if it is You, tell me to come out of the boat and walk on the water to meet You." "Come, Peter," Jesus said. And Peter recognized Jesus' voice.

Peter stepped out of the boat and onto the water. He walked a short way on the surface of the water just like Jesus! But when Peter looked away from Jesus and down at the big waves, he felt the strong winds blowing and was afraid of the dark sea beneath him. Peter began to sink into the water. He shouted, "Save me, Jesus! Help me!"

Immediately, Jesus went to Peter, grabbed his hand, and pulled him out of the water. "Peter," Jesus said, "why where you afraid? Why did you not trust Me?" Then they climbed up in the boat and the storm stopped.

Jesus' other disciples saw all of this and were astonished. They all said, "Jesus, You are truly God's own Son."

Jairus's Little Daughter

Luke 8:40–56

A father and mother in Capernaum had a twelve-year-old daughter who was very ill. The doctors did not know how to help her. The father, Jairus, was very worried and sad. But then he remembered Jesus. Jairus had heard a lot about Him and believed that Jesus could heal his little daughter.

Jairus rushed out of his house to find Jesus. This was easy to do because big crowds of people always surrounded Him. Jairus made his way through the crowd until he stood right in front of Jesus. Jairus begged, "Lord Jesus, please come to my house and place Your hands on my little girl. She is very ill, and I know You can heal her." So Jesus went with Jairus to his house.

Before they reached Jairus's house, though, a man came to him and said, "I am so sorry to tell you, but your daughter has died. Now there is no need for Jesus to come and heal her. She is already dead."

Then Jesus said to Jairus, "Do not worry. Your daughter is not dead; she is just sleeping. Trust that I will help you." And Jairus trusted Jesus and was not sad anymore.

When they arrived at Jairus's house, Jesus told the people who where there, "Go outside. She is only sleeping." Then He took Jairus and his wife into the room where the girl was lying in bed.

Jesus held the girl's hand and said, "Little girl, I say to you: Get up." Immediately, her heart started beating again, and she opened her eyes. She was not dead anymore. Jesus had healed her and brought her back to life! Her mother and father were overwhelmed with joy for what Jesus had done, and they thanked and praised God.

The Good Shepherd

Luke 15:1–7 & John 10:11

Jesus loved to tell stories and people loved listening to them. His stories always taught important things about who God is and what He is doing.

"Listen to this story about a shepherd," Jesus said one day.

"The shepherd had one hundred sheep and he took very good care of them. Every day, he led the sheep to fresh green grass and water so they had all they needed. The shepherd knew every one of his one hundred sheep so well that he could tell if they were doing well or if some of them were about to get ill.

"The sheep learned to stay close to the shepherd because they knew everything would be fine as long as they were in his sight. Every evening when they returned home, the shepherd carefully counted all his sheep to be sure they were all there. Then he locked them behind fences so they would be safe from the wild animals for the night.

"But one evening, as the shepherd counted his sheep, he realized that one was missing. He counted ninety-nine, so he knew one sheep was lost somewhere. It was now getting dark, but the shepherd knew he had to leave the ninety-nine sheep inside the fence and go out to find the one sheep that was missing.

"The shepherd went out searching in the dark wilderness. As the sun was setting, the shepherd went further and further away to find his lost sheep. Then, suddenly, he heard the sheep bleating and he rushed to find it. When he found the sheep, he placed it on his shoulders and carried it all the way back home. The shepherd was very happy because his sheep that had been lost was found again."

Jesus then said, "I told you this story to help you understand that God is exactly like this good shepherd who loves his sheep. If any person sins and strays from God, He will search for that person and bring him back to Him no matter what it requires. And, just like the good shepherd in the story, God is very happy when that person comes back to Him. God's joy is even greater than the shepherd's because people are so much more valuable to God than sheep are."

The Lost Son Comes Home

Luke 15:11–32

Jesus told another story about being lost and found. It was about a wealthy man who had two grown sons. The younger son wanted to leave his father and his home. He wanted to go explore the world and live on his own.

The younger son said, "Father, you promised to give me part of your money someday. Let me have it now so I can explore the world and have fun." The father was sad that his son wanted to leave home, but he did as his son asked and gave the money to him. The younger son then went far away to live in another country.

At first, the son had many new friends because he spent his money on them, and they went to parties all the time. It was an easy life. But then the son ran out of money. When his new friends realized this, they went to find someone else to be friends with. They left the son alone and gave him no help at all.

The younger son then found a job feeding pigs. It was very hard work, and the son was so hungry he wanted to eat the food he fed to the pigs. He was very sad, and he was afraid to go back home because he had disappointed his father and had spent all his money.

But one day, the son said, "The servants who work for my father have more food than I have here in this pig pen. I will go back home and ask my father if I can become a servant and work for him."

With that, the younger son went back home to his father. When he was almost home, he saw his father running down the road to meet him. The kind father had been watching every day to see if he would come back, so he was very happy to see his son again.

The father hugged and kissed his son. The son said, "Father, I have wasted your money and I do not deserve to be your son anymore. But may I work as a servant here in your house?" The father answered, "No, you cannot be a servant. You are my son and I am so happy that you are home again. We will have a big party and celebrate that my son who was lost has come home to me again."

When Jesus told this story, people listened very closely. Jesus said that God is exactly like the father in this story. Even when we do wrong things and ignore God, we can be sure that we can always turn back to Him. We will always be His dear children, and God will always welcome us.

The Good Samaritan Neighbor

Luke 10:25–37

Many people asked Jesus questions to learn from Him. But some people were His enemies. They wanted to trick Him into saying something that was wrong or false. So, quite often, Jesus answered these tricky questions by telling a story.

One day, some of the religious leaders in Israel came to Jesus and said, "The most important law is to love God completely and love your neighbor as yourself. But who is our neighbor?" They hoped Jesus would give them a wrong answer so they could criticize Him.

Jesus answered their question by telling this story. A Jewish man traveled from Jerusalem to Jericho. To get there, he had to travel a very dangerous road. As he was walking, some robbers jumped on him, beat him up, and stole all of his money. They left the man lying beside the road. He was bleeding and could not walk, but the robbers did not care about him and left him to die.

After a little while, a priest from the temple in Jerusalem came by. You would expect that such a man would stop to help, but although he could see the man lying and bleeding, the priest hurried on his way and did not stop to help the poor man.

A little later, another man, a Levite, came by and saw the injured man (a Levite was a priest who worked in the Jerusalem temple by helping with many practical things). Again, you would expect that a Levite who worked in God's temple would help the man who was hurt so badly. But he also looked the other way and did not stop.

After a while, a third man came along. This man was from Samaria.
Jewish people and Samaritan people were enemies. They usually stayed
away from each other. But when this Samaritan man saw the bleeding
man, he stopped his donkey and got off. He gave the injured man some
water and cleaned his wounds. Then he took the man to a nearby town
and found an inn.

The Samaritan man gave money to the innkeeper and said, "Take care of this man. I will pay whatever it costs for him to get well again."

After telling this story, Jesus asked, "Tell Me, which of these men acted like a good neighbor to the man who was hurt?" The people listening to Jesus answered, "The one who helped him, the man from Samaria." And Jesus said, "Then you should also be kind to everyone you meet, even to your enemies."

The Farmer and the Good Soil

Matthew 13:1–23

Jesus once told a story about a farmer who was planting his crop. With his big bag of seeds, the farmer went out to his field and tossed the seeds here and there, all over his field. This was the way farmers in those days would plant crops. Some of the seeds fell on the path where people and animals walked every day. The ground there was hard, and the seeds could not grow roots into the soil. Birds came and ate the seeds.

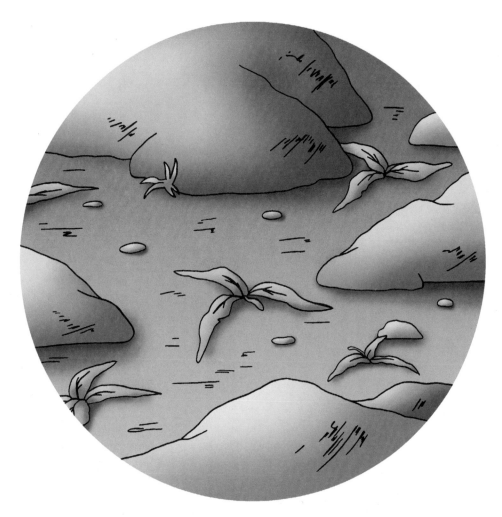

Some of the other seeds fell where the ground was covered with stones and had only a thin layer of soil. As soon as the sun and the rain came, the seeds started to grow. But the roots of the little plants could not grow deeply enough into the soil. In the heat of the bright sun, the plants quickly dried out and died.

Still other seeds fell in places where weeds and thorns grew. The seeds began to take root here too. But the weeds and the thorns were very thick and grew faster than the new, little plants. The weeds took all the sunlight and water, and the new plants lasted only a few days before they died.

The rest of the seeds fell on good soil where there were no stones, no weeds, and no thorns. The plants put down deep roots and quickly grew big and tall and strong. The farmer had a wonderful harvest from the seeds that fell in the good ground.

When Jesus finished this story, His disciples asked what it meant. Jesus told them, "This story is really about how people listen to what I say. The field is like the world we live in, and the seeds are My words. The birds, the soil covered with stones, and the weeds and thorns are like different people and how they listen to My words. Some people don't listen at all because their hearts are hard like the ground along the path. Other people listen carefully at first, but then quickly lose interest. They are like the soil filled with stones. The third kind of people are like the soil with weeds and thorns. They start out being very excited about My words, but after a little while, they start to worry about many things. They worry about money and having enough food; all their worries fill them up so much that their love for God dies."

"Finally, there are people who are like the good soil in the story. They listen to what I teach them about God. And God's love grows in their hearts every day, just like a strong plant that grows a little day by day. These people are filled with true joy because they believe in Me and live by My words."

The Treasure and the Beautiful Pearl

Matthew 13:44–46

Jesus once told two short stories about God's kingdom. A worker was plowing a field that belonged to someone else. Suddenly, his plow struck something very hard. The man stopped plowing and started digging in the ground to find out what it was. He thought that it was probably just a big rock and wanted to remove it from the field so he could keep plowing.

But what a surprise! There, in the field, was a box filled with a costly treasure. Quickly, the man covered the box back up with dirt and buried the treasure in the field. Then he rushed to town, where he sold everything he owned so he would have enough money to buy the field. He used all of his money to pay the owner for the field. Now the treasure that was buried there was his, and he was filled with joy.

Another man bought and sold pearls. Everywhere he went, he looked for beautiful and expensive pearls that he could buy and then sell again to make money.

One day, the man saw a very special pearl. It was the most beautiful pearl he had ever seen. The man said to himself, "I must have this one perfect pearl. I will never sell it. I will always keep it for myself."

So, the man sold everything he had, including all of his other pearls, and he bought the one very special pearl. Now he was happier than he had ever been.

Jesus told these stories to help people understand that God's kingdom is worth more than anything else in this world. It is the most precious treasure we could ever find. It is worth giving up everything else in this life.

The Lord's Prayer

Matthew 6:10–14 & Luke 11:2–4

One day, the disciples asked Jesus, "Lord, would You teach us how to pray?" He answered them by teaching them how to pray to God, our Father, everyday:

Our Father in heaven,
hallowed be Your name.
Your Kingdom come,
Your will be done,
on earth as in heaven.
Give us today our daily bread.
Forgive us our sins,
as we forgive those who sin against us.
Lead us not into temptation,
but deliver us from evil.
For Yours is the kingdom and the power and the glory.
Forever and ever. Amen

Lazarus, Wake Up!

John 11:1–44

Jesus often visited two sisters who lived in a town called Bethany. Their names were Martha and Mary. They had a brother named Lazarus, who was also Jesus' friend. One day, Lazarus became very sick. Mary and Martha sent a message to Jesus to come and see Lazarus and heal him. When Jesus heard that his good friend was sick, He said something strange. "Lazarus is not going to die," Jesus said. "He is only sleeping. And I will come and wake him up when I get back to Bethany."

By the time Jesus finally came to Bethany, Lazarus had already died. He had been in the tomb for four days. When Martha heard Jesus was near, she went out to meet Him and said, "Lord, if You had only been here sooner, Lazarus would not have died." But Jesus said, "Your brother will rise from the dead. Take Me to where Lazarus has been put to rest."

Mary, Martha, and some of their friends took Jesus to the grave
where Lazarus had been placed. There was a big stone in front of the
entrance. "Here is where Lazarus is buried," they said. When Jesus
saw the grave where His good friend lay dead, He cried. Then He
commanded the big stone to be pushed out of the away.

Jesus prayed to God. Then, with a loud voice, Jesus shouted, "Lazarus! Lazarus, come out here!" And Lazarus, wrapped with pieces of cloth, came walking out of the grave. He had died, but Jesus made him alive again!

All who saw this were completely astonished to see that God had given Jesus the power to raise Lazarus from the dead.

Jesus and Children

Luke 18:15–17

Jesus often showed that He has a very special, loving heart for children.
One day, some mothers tried to bring their little children to Jesus.
They wanted Jesus to put His hands on them and bless them. But the
disciples tried to keep the children away from Him. They thought Jesus
was much too busy with more important things and did not have time
for little children.

But when Jesus saw the disciples trying to send the children away, He said, "No! You must not keep these little children away from Me. I tell you this: If you are not like these small children, you will never enter God's kingdom. Let the little children come to Me, for they belong to God." And Jesus received the children and put His hands on them and blessed them.

Zacchaeus Was a Little Man

Luke 19:1–10

A man named Zacchaeus lived in Jericho. He working as a tax collector for King Herod. No one liked Herod, and therefore, people did not like tax collectors either. They especially didn't like Zacchaeus because he often cheated people and made them pay more taxes than they owed. Then he kept the extra money for himself.

Zacchaeus was a very little man. When he heard that Jesus was coming through Jericho, he went out to the street to see Him. But Zacchaeus was not tall enough to see over the crowd of people. So he climbed up in a tall tree where he could sit and watch Jesus. Now Zacchaeus could see Jesus coming toward them.

Everyone was surprised when Jesus stopped at the tree where Zacchaeus was. Jesus looked up and said, "Zacchaeus, come down. Today I want to eat dinner at your house." Zacchaeus quickly came down from the tree and took Jesus and the disciples to his house.

Zacchaeus was so happy Jesus wanted to come and have dinner with him. He knew he was a bad person, cheating people when he collected tax money from them. He could not understand that Jesus had come to his house because he was a sinner.

Zacchaeus listened carefully to Jesus' words about forgiveness. Then he said, "From now on, I want do what is right. I'm going to give half of my money to poor people. And I will pay back anyone I have cheated." Jesus was very happy with this and said, "Zacchaeus, I have come to save people exactly like you."

Entering Jerusalem

Matthew 21:1–11

When it was time to celebrate the Passover, Jesus traveled to Jerusalem to be with His disciples. Along the way to Jerusalem, Jesus sent two of His disciples into a small town. "Go into the town where you will see a donkey and her colt," He said to them. "Bring the colt to Me. If anyone asks you what you are doing, tell them 'The Lord needs it.' "

When the disciples came to the village, they found a donkey and her colt, just like Jesus said they would. When they took the colt, some men came and said, "Why are you taking the colt? It is not yours!" The disciples answered, "The Lord needs it." The men knew that Jesus needed the colt, so they let the disciples have it.

The disciples put their coats on the back of the colt, and Jesus got on and rode the colt. The disciples gathered around Him and they all entered the city of Jerusalem.

Word spread quickly that Jesus had come to Jerusalem and people ran to see Him. They cut leafy branches from palm trees and waved the branches like flags. People lay their coats across the road in front of Him and put other branches on the path.

The people of Jerusalem celebrated Jesus' coming. They hoped He would be their new king and throw out the Roman soldiers. They shouted, "Blessed is He who comes in the name of the Lord! Hosanna in the highest!"

This day is called Palm Sunday.

A Very Special Meal

Mark 14:12–26

Jesus and the disciples had come to Jerusalem to celebrate the Passover together. Passover was a time for Jewish people to remember how God had helped Moses and the Israelites escape from Pharaoh in Egypt. Jesus and His disciples met in a house to celebrate the Passover meal. During the meal, Jesus took some of the bread and thanked God for it. Then He gave bread to each of the disciples. "This is My body," He told them.

While they were eating, Jesus said something strange. "One of you has made an evil plan against Me and is going to help My enemies." The disciples were very surprised to hear this and wondered who among them would do such a wicked thing. Jesus then took a piece of bread, dipped it in some sauce, and handed the bread to Judas. He said, "Judas, go and do what you have to do." Without saying a word, Judas got up from his seat, left the room, and went into the night. Only Jesus and Judas knew what the evil plan was about.

Next, Jesus took a cup of the wine. He prayed and thanked God for it, and told the disciples to drink some of the wine. "This is My blood. It is given for you for the forgiveness of sins." Jesus told them, "I cannot be with you much longer. When I am no longer here, you shall eat bread and drink wine together like this meal we are having. When you do, remember Me and everything I have taught you." Jesus knew that it was almost time for Him to suffer and die in Jerusalem. But the disciples could not yet understand what was going to happen.

In the Garden of Gethsemane

Mark 14:32–51

When they finished the meal, Jesus and His disciples went to a garden in Jerusalem. The garden was called Gethsemane. Jesus said to the disciples, "Please, stay awake and pray with Me tonight." But the disciples were tired and fell asleep. Jesus was all alone as He prayed.

While Jesus was praying to God, Judas betrayed Him. Judas went to Jesus' enemies and told them where they could find and arrest Jesus. They sent out soldiers, and Judas led them into the garden where Jesus was praying. Judas said, "There will be other men with Jesus and it is dark and difficult to see who is who. I will walk up to Jesus and kiss Him." In this way, the soldiers would know which man to arrest. When Judas and the soldiers found Jesus in the garden, Judas went right up to Him and gave Him a kiss on the cheek. Then the soldiers grabbed Jesus.

But Peter saw what was going on and immediately drew his sword to protect Jesus from the soldiers. Peter hit one of the soldiers and cut off his ear. But Jesus said, "No, Peter, it is not right for you to draw your sword." Jesus put the soldier's ear back on again and the soldier was completely healed. Then Jesus was taken away by the soldiers.

Jesus before the High Priest and Pilate

Mark 14:53–65; Mark 15:1–15

The soldiers took Jesus to the high priest's house. There, they asked Jesus questions all night long. "This man claims to be God's Son," they said. "But it is not the truth. He is falsely claiming to be God. But He is a liar and He must face the toughest punishment. He must be put to death."

But the high priest could not sentence Jesus to death; only the Roman governor could do that. So the next morning, Jesus was taken to the Roman governor, Pilate. Jesus' enemies asked Pilate to have Jesus put to death. Pilate could see that Jesus was a good man and had not broken any law. But everyone shouted louder and louder, "This man must die." Pilate was afraid all the people would start fighting, so to calm the people down, he ordered Jesus to be taken outside of the city and put to death on a cross.

The Cross

Matthew 27:31–55

The soldiers crucified Jesus.

Two robbers also hung on crosses, one on each side of Jesus. Although it was the middle of the afternoon, the sun disappeared and a great darkness came over the land. "It is finished," Jesus said. Then He breathed His last breath. Jesus died.

To some people, it may have looked as if everything Jesus said and did was pointless. But the reason Jesus died in this way was because His sacrifice was God's plan from the very beginning. Because Jesus is God's true Son, He always knew it would be this way. By His death, Jesus took on Himself the punishment for all the sin that people have done and still are doing. Jesus took every person's punishment and died for us. He did this to take away our sins so we will not be judged by God for our sins.

But for Jesus' friends who watched it, this was the saddest day in their life. They did not understand what was going on. They wondered why God allowed Jesus to die. But this was going to change very soon.

Jesus Is Alive!

Mark 16:1–8; Matthew 28:1–10; John 20:1–10; Luke 24:1–53

Jesus was taken down from the cross and buried in a cave. A huge rock was placed right in front of it. But early in the morning on the third day after Jesus died, a mighty angel went to the cave and rolled away the stone from the entrance. And then Jesus stepped out! He was no longer dead. He was alive again! God brought Jesus back to life!

A little later that same morning, two of Jesus' disciples, Peter and John, and a woman named Mary Magdalene came to see the cave where Jesus had been buried. But when they got there, they could see that the big stone had been rolled away and Jesus was no longer there. Peter went inside the cave and found Jesus' clothes lying on the stone where His dead body had been placed. Peter and John went back home and wondered what to do.

Mary Magdalene stayed behind. When she went up to the cave, she saw two angels. One of them said to her, "Why are you looking for Jesus here? Jesus is no longer here. He has risen from the dead and is alive again, just like He told you." Mary believed what the angel said and she was no longer sad because she knew Jesus was alive. Then Jesus Himself spoke to Mary and told her the truth—He was alive! Mary was so happy. She went back to tell everybody the wonderful news.

This is the day we know as Easter, and we celebrate it joyfully.

Later that evening, while the disciples were together in a house, Jesus came into the room and talked with them. The disciples touched Him to make sure He really was alive. Now they were no longer sad. They were full of joy and happiness.

After this, Jesus showed Himself to many other people too. All people who saw Jesus knew for sure that He was alive again and that God had raised Him from the dead.

The Big Catch of Fish

John 21:1–12

One night, soon after Jesus had died and rose from the grave, the disciples went back to work as fishermen. They had worked all night, but they hadn't caught any fish. Now the sun began to rise. They could see a man walking along the shore. The man called to them and said, "Drop your net on the other side of the boat. That is where the fish are."

Without knowing yet who the man was, the disciples obeyed and dropped their net into the water on the other side of the boat. When they pulled up the net again, it was so filled with fish that it almost burst. It was truly a miracle! John then said to Peter, "I am sure that man is Jesus!"

Peter knew then this was true. He was so excited that he could not wait to see Jesus and talk to Him. So Peter jumped right into the sea with all his clothes on! He swam to get to Jesus as fast as he could. The others came behind him in the boat, dragging the heavy nets full of fish.

Yes, the man on the beach was Jesus. He was sitting calmly by a fire and was cooking fish for His disciples. "Would you like some breakfast?" He asked them. Jesus wanted to spend time with the disciples. He wanted to teach them more about God, about the meaning of His crucifixion when He died, and about Easter when He rose from the dead. But first, Jesus just wanted to take good care of His friends and make sure they were not hungry.

Jesus Leaves Earth

Acts 1:6--1

When it was time for Him to leave earth, He took His disciples to a hill outside of Jerusalem. Jesus said, "It's time for Me to go back to heaven to be with My Father. After I'm back in heaven, you must go to Jerusalem and wait until I send My Spirit upon you. After that, you will go out everywhere in the world to tell people about Me and everything I have taught you during these years we have spent together."

When Jesus spoke these words, He began to rise from the earth. He went up and up, until a cloud covered Him and He went out of sight.

Jesus had gone back to heaven to be with God. For a long time, the disciples stood silently and looked up into the sky. They did not know what to think or say about this.

Suddenly, the disciples saw that two angels were standing beside them. The angels asked, "Why are you standing here looking up in the sky? Jesus has gone to heaven. One day, Jesus will come back again in the same way you have just now seen Him leave earth." Then the disciples returned to Jerusalem and stayed there, as Jesus had told them to do, waiting for His Holy Spirit to come to them.

Flames of Fire

Acts 2:1–13

A few weeks after Jesus returned to heaven, the disciples were gathered at a place close to the big temple in Jerusalem. The temple was filled with people because it was a very special Jewish holiday. Every year Jews from all over the world traveled to Jerusalem to celebrate this holiday in the temple.

Suddenly, a loud noise filled the place where the disciples were. It sounded like a mighty wind. A small flame of fire appeared above each of the disciples' heads. This was what Jesus had promised them when He left the earth. It was God's Holy Spirit, which now came upon them. The gift of the Holy Spirit meant that the disciples were able to spread the Good News, the teaching that Jesus had been preparing them for. This was the sign for the disciples that it was time for them to start telling people about Jesus.

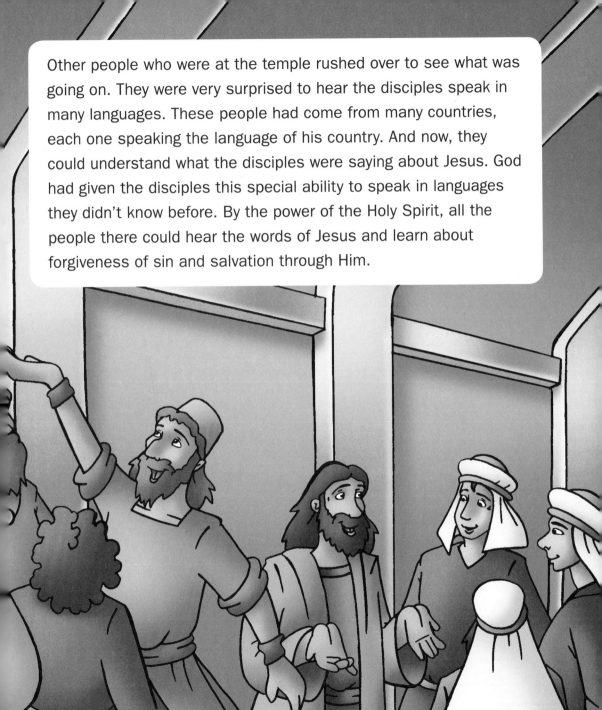

Other people who were at the temple rushed over to see what was going on. They were very surprised to hear the disciples speak in many languages. These people had come from many countries, each one speaking the language of his country. And now, they could understand what the disciples were saying about Jesus. God had given the disciples this special ability to speak in languages they didn't know before. By the power of the Holy Spirit, all the people there could hear the words of Jesus and learn about forgiveness of sin and salvation through Him.

Peter and John in the Temple

Acts 3:1-10

On another day, the two good friends, Peter and John, were on their way to the temple to pray and to teach people about Jesus. Right outside the entrance to the temple, they saw a man who could not walk. This man always sat just outside of the temple begging people for money so he could buy food and clothes. He had been begging since he was a child.

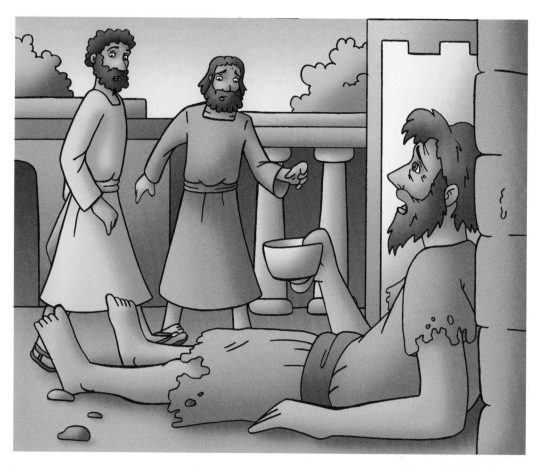

When Peter and John came near, the man asked them for some money. Peter and John looked at him and felt sorry for him. "We don't have silver or gold," Peter said to him. "But we will be happy to give you what we do have. In Jesus' name, I say to you: Stand up and start walking!" And Peter took the man's hand and helped him up on his feet.

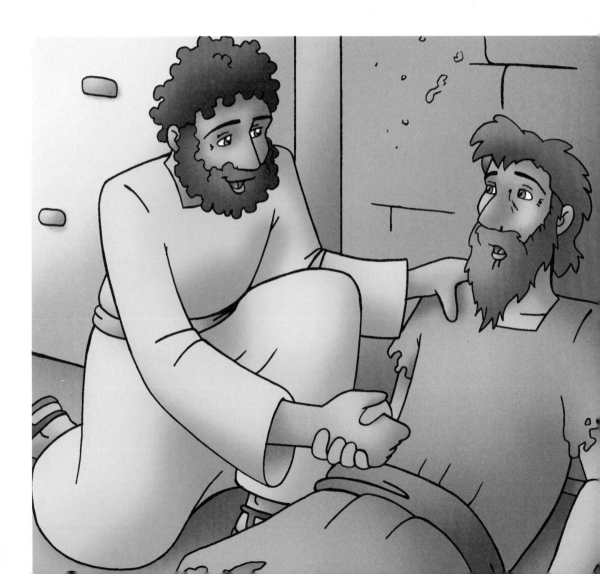

Immediately, an amazing power rushed through the man and he felt strength in his legs. Now he could walk and jump. Dancing and singing, he went into the temple to praise and thank God for healing him through Peter.

Peter then said, "It is Jesus' power, not mine, which has healed the man." And all the people who saw the miracle with their own eyes were completely amazed about what God had done. So they all started to praise and thank God because the lame man could walk again.

When Saul Became Paul

Acts 9:1–19

After the disciples had received God's Holy Spirit, more and more
people became followers of Jesus, or as we say today, Christians. But it
was not easy back then to be a Christian. Many of the disciples and the
first Christians were put into jail. There was one man in Jerusalem who
especially did not like Christians. His name was Saul. This man spent
most of his time catching Christians and putting them in jail.

Saul traveled to many places, looking for Christians to arrest. When he heard that there were many Christians in the city of Damascus, he decided to go there to close the Christian churches and put the church leaders in jail. This city was far from Jerusalem, so it took him several days to walk there.

But as he was walking to Damascus, something happened that changed Saul completely. He had almost reached the city when, suddenly, a bright light began to shine on him. The light came from the sky, and it was so bright that Saul could not see or keep his eyes open. Saul fell to the ground and realized the light had left him blind.

Just then Saul heard a voice from heaven: "Saul, Saul. Why are you fighting Me?" Saul was shocked and asked, "Who are you?" The voice answered, "I am Jesus." He told Saul to go into the city and wait there. Later, Saul would understand what Jesus wanted him to do.

Saul was still blind, so his friends guided him into the city. They took him by the hand and led him to a house in Damascus. Saul stayed in this house and prayed for three days and nights. Then God sent an old man named Ananias to talk to Saul. Ananias touched Saul's eyes and all at once he was able to see again. Ananias explained that God wanted Saul to be a leader in the Christian Church. God wanted Saul to spend the rest of his life following Jesus and teaching others about Him.

That same day, Saul was baptized in Jesus' name. Then he changed his name to make it clear to everyone that he was beginning a new life as a Christian. He was no longer an enemy of Christians. He now was called "Paul."

He continued to travel to many places, but now he told everyone he met about Jesus and what it means to be a Christian. The man who once had caught and put the Christians in jail now became one of the leaders of the Church.

Paul in Prison

Acts 16:16–34

It was not easy for Paul to live as a Christian. He had many enemies who lied about him, beat him up, and did all kinds of evil things to him. Paul was put in prison several times. One time, he was in prison with his good friend Silas. Even there, they continued to tell about God. One night, in their prison cell, Paul and Silas were singing about God and praying to Him.

It was around midnight, and as Paul and Silas were singing, a mighty earthquake struck the prison. The thick walls began to shake and all the doors broke open so it was possible for all the prisoners to escape. Paul and Silas also had a chance to escape, but all the prisoners stayed where they were.

The man in charge of the prison was very afraid. If anyone escaped, he was responsible and would be punished. Maybe he would even be put to death because the prisoners had escaped. But Paul called out to the man and said, "Don't worry, everyone is still here. No one has escaped."

The man rushed into the prison cells. He looked around and, just as Paul said, no one was gone. This man knew then that Paul and Silas believed in Jesus. He had heard them, as they were singing and praying. He said to Paul, "I want to be a Christian. Can you tell me more about Jesus?" He then brought Peter and Silas from the prison to his home, where his wife gave them something to eat. Paul baptized the man and his whole family in Jesus' name. Now they were Christians too.

Shipwrecked!

Acts 24–28

Paul had once again been put in prison, and this time he was to stay there for several years. Then Paul was reminded that because he was a Roman, it was possible for him to complain about his arrest to the Roman emperor. So the soldiers put Paul on a ship that was sailing to Rome. Some of Paul's friends also came along on this long boat journey.

At the beginning of the voyage, the weather was nice and the sea was calm. But then the wind became stronger and stronger, and it was difficult for the captain to steer the boat. Paul warned the captain. "Don't go any further," Paul said. "We will all die if you continue." But the captain and the soldiers decided to continue on the voyage anyway.

Right after this, a very strong storm came and big waves hit the ship. The ship was rolling forth and back, and all the sailors were afraid the ship would sink. There was nothing the sailors could do to control the ship. For three days, the ship was caught in the storm. Everyone began losing hope that they would survive and see land again.

Paul then called out to everyone and said, "You should have listened to my warning, but don't give up hope. God has told me that we all will survive and reach land. I trust in God." The next morning the weather was much better and the wind not so strong. The sailors gained control over the ship. Now they could see land, so they set course toward the shore.

But just as they set sail, the ship ran aground. Big waves hit the ship and began to break it apart. Everyone had to get off before it sank. The soldiers wondered what to do with the prisoners. They even thought about killing the prisoners, but the soldiers decided to give everyone a chance to swim to shore. Those who could not swim grabbed on to some wood from the ship. And just like God had promised Paul, all of the two hundred and fifty men who were on the ship swam to shore and were safe.

They had reached an island called Malta and had to stay there for more than three months until a new ship came to take them to Rome. Finally, after a very long and dangerous journey, Paul arrived in Rome. There he spent a lot of time telling the people he met about Jesus. People from all over the world came to Rome, so the message of Jesus spread quickly throughout the world. Paul also visited many Christians in Rome and told them all he had learned about God.

God's Wonderful City

Paul and the two disciples, Peter and John, wrote many letters to different churches all over the world. They wrote letters to teach other Christians about Jesus, His life, death, and resurrection, and about God and His love. These letters were really appreciated by the Christians. Every time they gathered in church, they took these letters and read them over and over again.

The disciple John had been one of Jesus' closest friends. He lived
longer than any of the disciples, and became a very old man. John
spent all his life telling about Jesus, and he traveled to far away
countries to do so. Late in his life, John was forced to stay all alone
on a small island called Patmos. In this way, the enemies of Christians
hoped he would not be able to continue to speak about Jesus anymore.
But it did not happen that way.

One day, John had a very special experience. Suddenly, he could see right into heaven, where God is. He could see Jesus dressed in a splendid white robe, and he saw God's throne surrounded by a rainbow. All around it, he could see angels, and they were singing, "Holy, holy, holy is God the Almighty." Later, some of the angels showed John what will happen in the future. John wrote down all of what he saw and heard. Then, he sent letters about it to his friends so they could tell other Christians what John had seen and been told about the future.

When John was looking into heaven, he saw a very special city. It was the most beautiful city he had ever seen; everything was covered with gold and pearls. John saw the city where God and Jesus live. Even the streets were made of gold. In the middle of the city was a beautiful river and along the river were trees. The most wonderful fruits were growing on these trees, and when people eat the fruit, they live forever.

Heaven is a place where there is no more pain, suffering, sickness, or death. Only good and wonderful things happen there. Jesus is waiting for us to be with Him there when we leave this world. He is preparing a home for us, and there is plenty of room for everyone. And we will live there forever, with Jesus and God and all other believers.